I0415549

Art and promotional text (c) Booklife 2010
ISBN 978-1-105-81100-5

Coast Guard Publication 1

U.S. Coast Guard: America's Maritime Guardian

Originally published
May 2009
Commercially reprinted
March 2010

THE COMMANDANT OF THE UNITED STATES COAST GUARD

Washington, D.C. 20593-0001
May 1, 2009

Commandant's Letter of Promulgation

For over two centuries the U. S. Coast Guard has safeguarded our Nation's maritime interests in the heartland, in the ports, at sea, and around the globe. We protect the maritime economy and the environment, we defend our maritime borders, and we save those in peril. This history has forged our character and purpose as America's Maritime Guardian—*Always Ready* for all hazards and all threats.

I am proud to introduce the first revision of *Coast Guard Publication 1, U.S. Coast Guard: America's Maritime Guardian* (Pub 1). Since its original printing in 2002, Pub 1 has served as our capstone doctrine. It defines our principles and culture. It describes our history, our missions, our purpose, and our Guardian Ethos. It communicates who and what the Coast Guard is, what we do, and how we accomplish our missions.

I expect all Coast Guard members to read and become familiar with Pub 1. Embrace the lessons from the past so you can adapt to our dynamic environment and improve our future mission performance. Discuss it with your shipmates and use it as a fundamental building block to educate our newest members just entering the Service. A common understanding of our guiding principles and beliefs will strengthen us as an organization.

For anyone curious about the Coast Guard, this one document will give you a sound understanding of our unique organization and what we offer to our Nation and the world. This document belongs to every member of the Coast Guard family—active duty, reservist, civilian, and auxiliarist. I am confident it will help us meet the maritime challenges of the 21st century.

Semper Paratus!

THAD W. ALLEN
Admiral, U.S. Coast Guard

A few armed vessels, judiciously stationed at the entrances of our ports,
might at a small expense be made useful sentinels of the laws.

— Alexander Hamilton, the first Secretary of the Treasury
Federalist No. 12, The Utility of the Union in Respect to Revenue
From the New York Packet, November 27, 1787
Earliest recorded reference to what would become the U.S. Coast Guard

It had the desired effect.

— Captain John Faunce, USRCS
Commanding Officer, *USRC Harriet Lane*
Comment in Harper's Weekly about firing the first naval shot
of the Civil War in Charleston, South Carolina

Did they get off?

— Signalman First Class Douglas Munro, USCG,
Medal of Honor recipient
Inquiring of the nearly 500 Marines he helped evacuate,
just before dying of wounds he suffered in the effort

These poor, plain men, dwellers upon the lonely sands of Hatteras, took their
lives in their hands, and, at the most imminent risk crossed the most
tumultuous sea...and all for what?
That others might live to see home and friends.

— Annual Report of the U.S. Life-Saving Service, 1885

The lighthouse and the lightship appeal to the interests and better instinct of
man because they are symbolic of never ceasing watchfulness, of steadfast
endurance in every exposure, of widespread helpfulness.

— George R. Putnam, the first Commissioner of Lighthouses
U.S. Lighthouse Service, 1906-1935

Having fought as a part of the Navy in all our wars,
and taking an especial pride in being fully prepared to perform credible service
in the Navy whenever called upon, the officers and men of the Coast Guard
are inspired not only by the high traditions and fine history of their own
service, but also by the splendid traditions, history, and indoctrination of the
United States Navy. They have thus two rich heritages to be proud of and two
standards of the same lofty character to live up to.

— Rear Admiral F. C. Billard, USCG
Commandant of the Coast Guard, 1924-1932
U.S. Naval Institute Proceedings, May 1929

TABLE OF CONTENTS

Introduction

In 1790, the First Congress of the United States established a small maritime law enforcement agency to assist in collecting the new Nation's customs duties. For the next eight years, this Revenue Marine (later called the Revenue Cutter Service) was the Nation's only naval force and thus was soon assigned military duties. Over time, the Revenue Cutter Service either merged with or absorbed other federal agencies. The Service acquired new responsibilities based upon its ability to perform them with existing assets and minimal disruption to its other duties. In some cases, the Service absorbed other agencies because their maritime responsibilities were seen as intersecting with or complementing its own. The result is today's U.S. Coast Guard—a unique force that carries out an array of civil and military responsibilities touching almost every facet of the maritime environment of the United States.

What makes the Coast Guard unique is that in executing our diverse missions we harmonize seemingly contradictory mandates. We are charged at once to be police officers, sailors, warriors, humanitarians, regulators, stewards of the environment, diplomats, and guardians of the coast. Thus, we are **military, multi-mission, and maritime.**

Coast Guard members and the units in which they serve are always ready to act across the entire range of Coast Guard missions. But as a practical matter, some responsibilities demand more time, effort, and resources than others. Emphasis on specific missions should not, however, cause us to lose focus on the broad roles of the Coast Guard and the way in which these roles affect how our Service is organized, equipped, and conducts operations. Indeed, it is the fluid multi-mission nature of the Coast Guard that is our greatest strength and our greatest value to the American people. Each Coast Guard member must understand our Service as a whole. This document is designed to provide context for that understanding.

Publication 1 (Pub 1) explains what we do and who we are. It describes the fundamental roles and forces of today's Coast Guard. In keeping with our military nature, Pub 1 is consistent with Joint Publication 1 (JP 1), which is the capstone doctrine for unified action by the Armed Forces of the United

States. It also aligns with Naval Doctrine Publication 1 (NDP 1), which describes how the U.S. Naval Services operate as an integrated force across a range of military operations. However, while we are a military service at all times, defense readiness is only one of the Coast Guard's 11 missions. Thus, Pub 1 describes the full military, multi-mission, and maritime nature of our Service.

This document traces our history to explain how the Coast Guard acquired its diverse mission set. It explains the unique characteristics and qualities—derived from our history, roles, and missions—that collectively define who we are. Finally, it lays out principles of operations that flow from our particular organizational nature and identity. In other words, it also describes how we do things.

The principles of operation discussed in this publication are Coast Guard doctrine; that is, they are fundamental concepts that guide our actions in support of the Nation's objectives. Rooted in our history and distilled of hard won experience, they provide a shared interpretation of that experience. This, in turn, provides a common starting point for thinking about future directions. Together with training and experience, this shared outlook leads to consistent behavior, mutual confidence, and more effective collective action—without constraining initiative.

Because this doctrine is rooted in history, it is enduring. But it also evolves in response to changes in the political and strategic landscape, lessons from current operations, and the introduction of new technologies. Doctrine influences the way policy and plans are developed, forces are organized, trained and employed, and equipment is procured and maintained. It promotes unity of purpose, guides professional judgment, and enables Coast Guard active duty, reserve, civilian, and auxiliary members to best fulfill their responsibilities. Pub 1 tells us how we became—and why we are—**America's Maritime Guardian.**

Chapter One

America's Maritime Guardian

*A*merica's enduring maritime interests—its reliance on the seas for commerce, sustenance, and defense—have changed little since colonial days. The U.S. Coast Guard exists to address these interests. The United States is a maritime country, with extensive interests in the seas around us and far beyond. Having 95,000 miles of shoreline and nearly 3.4 million square miles of Exclusive Economic Zones (EEZ), the United States will always remain tied to the sea. The seas link the Nation with world trade and commerce.

They allow us to project military power beyond our shores to protect important U.S. interests, and to assist allies or friends. Regrettably, however, the seas also serve as highways for criminal and terrorist threats that honor no national borders.

The Coast Guard is one of the five military services which make up the Armed

USCGC *Adak* stands guard over the Statue of Liberty.

Forces of the United States of America. As such, we exist to defend and preserve the United States as a free nation. We also protect important interests of the United States— the personal safety and security of our population; the marine transportation system and critical infrastructure; our natural and economic resources; and the territorial integrity of our nation— from both internal and external threats, natural and man-made. We protect these interests in U.S. ports and inland waterways, along the coasts, on international waters, and in any other maritime region where they may be at risk. Since 1915, when the Coast Guard was established by law as an armed force, we have been a military, multi-mission, maritime force offering a unique blend of military, law enforcement, humanitarian, regulatory, and diplomatic capabilities. These capabilities underpin our three broad roles: **maritime safety, maritime security, and maritime stewardship.**[1]

Each Coast Guard role is composed of several missions. The 11 missions listed in Figure 1 have been statutorily assigned to us by the Congress, acting on behalf of the American people. However, most Coast Guard missions support more than one role. For example, our aids to navigation mission primarily supports our maritime stewardship role by preventing pollution from vessel groundings and collisions, while facilitating the movement of people and goods. But this mission also supports our maritime safety role by preventing accidents, injuries, and deaths. These interwoven roles and complementary missions call for Coast Guard personnel and resources that are similarly multi-mission capable. This characteristic of our people and our platforms—their ability to perform multiple missions—brings greater effectiveness, insight, and agility to bear in any situation. It is a fundamental source of the Coast Guard's strength.

Protecting U.S. Maritime Interests
Through Multi-Mission Integration

Figure 1

Following the terrorist attacks of September 11, 2001, Congress passed the Homeland Security and the Maritime Transportation Security Acts of 2002, and transferred the Coast Guard into the Department of Homeland Security (DHS). But these actions have not substantially altered the Service's roles and missions. Rather, these developments have brought increased emphasis to the importance of the Coast Guard's multimission work in protecting U.S. maritime borders and enforcing U.S. sovereignty over our coastal waters. As criminals and terrorists try to exploit or blend in with legitimate maritime activity, the Coast Guard's roles of **maritime safety, security, and stewardship** are increasingly recognized as interrelated and essential to our nation's layered security construct against all threats and all hazards.

> ## The Homeland Security Act of 2002
>
> **Created on November 25, 2002, the Department of Homeland Security (DHS) is assigned seven statutory missions. These mostly focus on preventing, responding to, or recovering from terrorist attacks on the U.S.**
>
> **But DHS also is charged with executing a wider array of activities essential to the safety and security of our citizens. Thus, one mission is to '[c]arry out all functions of [agencies] transferred to the Department.' This includes '...acting as a focal point regarding natural and manmade crises and emergency planning.'**
>
> **The Coast Guard directly supports all DHS missions. It provides DHS the broad authorities, capabilities, and partnerships necessary to accomplish its tasks in the maritime domain.**

Coast Guard Roles and Missions

Maritime Safety

A fundamental responsibility of the U.S. government is to safeguard the lives and safety of its citizens. In the maritime realm, this duty falls mainly to the Coast Guard. In partnership with other federal agencies, state, local, and tribal governments, marine industries, and individual mariners, we improve safety at sea through complementary programs of mishap prevention, search and rescue, and accident investigation.

> ### Maritime Safety Missions
>
> - **Marine Safety**
> - **Search and Rescue**

Coast Guard prevention activities include the development of standards and regulations, various types of plan review and compliance inspections, and a variety of safety programs designed to protect mariners.

The Coast Guard is America's voice in the International Maritime Organization (IMO), which promulgates measures to improve shipping safety, pollution prevention, mariner training, and certification standards. We develop and enforce vessel construction standards as well as domestic shipping and navigation regulations.

To ensure compliance, we review and approve plans for ship construction, repair, and alteration. We inspect vessels, mobile offshore drilling units, and marine facilities for safety. Our Port State Control program, aimed at eliminating substandard vessels from U.S. ports and waterways, is a key element. This program is critical since the majority of the passenger and cargo ships operating in U.S. waters are foreign flagged.

Nearly all Coast Guard prevention activities are designed to protect mariners. For example, our commercial fishing vessel safety programs are designed to safeguard commercial fishermen, many

of whom earn their living performing some of the most dangerous work in the world. We operate the International Ice Patrol to protect ships transiting the North Atlantic shipping lanes. We document and admeasure U.S. flag vessels. And, we license commercial mariners.

Coast Guard boarding team members prepare to perform a safety inspection on a fishing vessel. They check the overall condition of life rings, survival suits, and other safety and lifesaving equipment onboard.

America has approximately 17 million recreational boats.[2] As National Recreational Boating Safety Coordinator, the Coast Guard works to minimize loss of life, personal injury, property damage, and environmental harm associated with this activity. Our boating safety program involves public education programs, regulation of boat design and construction, approval of boating safety equipment, and vessel safety checks for compliance with federal and state safety requirements. The all-volunteer Coast Guard Auxiliary plays a central role in this program.

But the maritime domain is large and complex, and the sea is powerful and unforgiving. Despite our best efforts, mariners sometimes find themselves in harm's way. When they do, the Coast Guard has a long heritage and proud tradition of immediate response to save lives and property in peril. As the lead agency for maritime search and rescue (SAR) in U.S. waters, we coordinate the SAR efforts of afloat and airborne Coast Guard units with those of other federal, state, and local responders. We also partner with the world's merchant fleet to rescue mariners in distress around the globe through the Automated Mutual-assistance Vessel Rescue (AMVER) system. Using its Captain of the Port (COTP) authorities and responsibilities, the Coast Guard also coordinates response efforts on waterways after an incident or disaster.

UCSGC *Munro*, an HH-65 helicopter, and two HC-130 fixed-wing aircraft come to the rescue of the foundering container ship *Hyundai Seattle*, December 1994.

In addition to responding to a variety of maritime accidents and emergencies, we investigate their causes. We determine whether applicable laws have been violated, or whether changes should be made to improve safety through our prevention programs. This work is often done in coordination with the National Transportation Safety Board (NTSB).

Coast Guard activities in support of maritime safety are often inseparable from those we perform to protect the marine environment or secure the U.S. Marine Transportation System (MTS). A routine inspection for safety compliance may uncover a serious risk to the environment. Coast Guard vessel traffic services not only reduce the risk of vessel collisions, but also provide maritime domain awareness. This improves security. A buoy tender working an aid to navigation may immediately divert to a search and rescue case. The integration of *all* Coast Guard missions has saved many thousands of lives, helped secure our citizens, and contributed to our national economic and environmental well-being.

Maritime Security

Maritime law enforcement and border control are the oldest of the Coast Guard's numerous responsibilities. They date back to our founding as the Revenue Marine in 1790. The First Congress established the Revenue Marine specifically to patrol our coasts and seaports to frustrate smuggling and enforce the customs laws of the fledgling Republic. Over two centuries later, that early challenge has evolved into a global obligation for the maritime security of our nation. Our maritime law enforcement and border control duties require the interdiction of ships at sea. This core capability provides the foundation upon which today's broader and more complex maritime security mission set has been built.

> **Maritime Security Missions**
>
> • **Drug Interdiction**
>
> • **Migrant Interdiction**
>
> • **Defense Readiness**
>
> • **Ports, Waterways, and Coastal Security**

As the Nation's primary maritime law enforcement service, the Coast Guard enforces, or assists in enforcing, federal laws and treaties on waters under U.S. jurisdiction, and other international agreements on the high seas. We possess the civil authority to board any vessel subject to U.S. jurisdiction. Once aboard, we can inspect, search, inquire, and arrest. We wield this broad police power with prudence and restraint primarily to suppress violations of our drug, immigration, and fisheries laws, as well as to secure our nation from terrorist threats.

Members of a Coast Guard Law Enforcement Detachment transfer confiscated drugs from a captured self-propelled semi-submersible vessel to a U.S. Navy small boat. These semi-submersible vessels have such a low profile they are difficult to detect using radar or aircraft.

The Coast Guard is the designated lead agency for maritime drug interdiction under the National Drug

Control Strategy and the co-lead agency for air interdiction operations with U.S. Customs and Border Protection. As such, the Coast Guard defends America's seaward frontier against a torrent of illegal drugs. For more than three decades, our cutters and aircraft have forward deployed off South America and in the drug transit zone. They have intercepted thousands of tons of cocaine, marijuana, and other illegal drugs that otherwise would have found their way to America's streets.

Coast Guard undocumented migrant interdiction operations are law enforcement missions with an important humanitarian dimension. Migrants often take great risks and endure significant hardships in their attempts to flee their countries and enter the United States. In many cases, migrant vessels interdicted at sea are overloaded and unseaworthy, lack basic safety equipment, and are operated by inexperienced mariners. Many of the undocumented migrant cases we handle actually begin as search and rescue incidents. Once again, this illustrates the interweaving of our roles and missions. Between 1982 and 2007, we interdicted over 225,000 migrants mostly from Cuba, the Dominican Republic, and Haiti.

Crew members from *UCSGC Confidence* rescue undocumented migrants from a severely overcrowded vessel.

Throughout our history, the Coast Guard has served with the U.S. Navy to defend our nation. This began with the Quasi-War with France in 1798, and continued through the Civil War, the World Wars, Vietnam, the Persian Gulf War, and Operation Iraqi Freedom.

Today, as a critical component of the U.S. National Fleet, we maintain a high state of readiness to operate as a specialized service alongside the Navy and Marine Corps. The close relationship among our services has evolved over two centuries of cooperation. This enduring relationship is captured in the May 2008 agreement between the Secretaries of Defense and Homeland Security.

The agreement formalizes the use of Coast Guard competencies and resources in support of the National Military Strategy and other national-level defense and security strategies. It lists the following Coast Guard national defense capabilities:

- Maritime interception and interdiction;
- Military environmental response;
- Port operations, security, and defense;
- Theater security cooperation;
- Coastal sea control;
- Rotary wing air intercept;
- Combating terrorism; and
- Maritime Operational Threat Response support

These support the unified combatant commanders and require the Coast Guard to execute essential military operations in peacetime, crisis, and war.

Members of the Coast Guard's Maritime Safety and Security Teams employ bomb-sniffing dogs to improve port security.

Our domestic civil law enforcement and port security expertise are uniquely valuable today as combatant commanders work to build foreign nation capacity for security and governance. In recent years, combatant commanders have requested Coast Guard forces to conduct at-sea interception and anti-piracy operations, foreign liaison, and other supporting warfare tasks in all key theaters.

The Coast Guard has been responsible for the security of the ports and waterways of the United States during times of war since the enactment of the Espionage Act of 1917. After World War II, the Magnuson Act of 1950 assigned the Coast Guard an ongoing mission to safeguard U.S. ports, harbors, vessels, and waterfront facilities from accidents, sabotage, or other subversive acts.

Following the terrorist attacks of September 11, 2001, these authorities took on grave new importance. This includes denying terrorists the use of the U.S. maritime domain and the U.S. MTS to mount attacks on our territory, population, or critical infrastructure.

Our authorities were further strengthened with the passage of the Maritime Transportation Security Act of 2002. This designated Coast Guard Captains of the Port as the Federal Maritime Security Coordinators. The Coast Guard thus became the lead agency for coordinating all maritime security planning and operations in our ports and waterways. These activities encompass all efforts to prevent or respond to attacks.

Maritime security is a continuing theme running throughout our proud history of service to America. It requires a breadth of experience and skills—seamanship, diplomacy, legal expertise, and combat readiness. We have honed these skills for more than two centuries. No other federal agency offers this combination of law enforcement and military capabilities, together with the legal authorities to carry them out.

Maritime Stewardship

Our nation's waters are vital to its well-being and economy. The marine environment of the United States is one of the most valuable natural resources on Earth. It contains one-fifth of the world's fishery resources. It is also a region of extraordinary recreation, energy and mineral resources, and transportation activities. Finally, it is an inseparable part of our national heritage and daily fabric of life in our coastal communities.

Maritime Stewardship Missions

- **Living Marine Resources**

- **Marine Environmental Protection**

- **Other Law Enforcement (Fisheries)**

- **Aids to Navigation**

- **Ice Operations**

The Coast Guard's role in protecting natural resources dates to the 1820s when Congress tasked the Revenue Marine to protect federal stocks of Florida live oak trees. These trees were deemed critical to the security of our young nation because they provided the best wood for shipbuilding.

As the exploitation of the Nation's valuable marine resources—whales, furbearing animals, and fish—increased, we were given the duty to protect those resources as well. Today, U.S. waters support commercial and recreational fisheries worth more than $30 billion annually, and we serve as the primary agency for at-sea fisheries enforcement. The Coast Guard, in coordination with other federal and state agencies, enforces marine resource management and protection regimes to preserve healthy stocks of fish and other living marine resources.

A People's Republic of China Fisheries Law Enforcement Command (FLEC) officer, in cooperation with the U.S. Coast Guard, seizes a Chinese fishing vessel suspected of illegal high-seas drift net fishing.

In 1976, Congress passed what is now known as the Magnuson-Stevens Fishery Conservation and Management Act. By creating an EEZ, this legislation extended our exclusive rights out to 200 nautical miles for fisheries and other natural resources. The Coast Guard patrols these areas to uphold U.S. sovereignty and protect precious resources. Today, international fisheries agreements have extended U.S. jurisdiction to waters beyond the EEZ.

Our stewardship role has expanded to include enforcing laws intended to protect the environment for the common good. As a result, we safeguard sensitive marine habitats, mammals, and endangered species. We enforce laws protecting our waters from the discharge of oil, hazardous substances, and non-indigenous invasive species.

To do all this, the Coast Guard conducts a wide range of activities. These include education and prevention; law enforcement; emergency response and containment; and disaster recovery. We also provide mission critical command and control support for forces responding to environmental disasters in the maritime domain.

Under the National Contingency Plan, Coast Guard COTPs are the pre-designated Federal On-Scene Coordinators (FOSC) for oil and hazardous substance incidents in all coastal and some inland areas. The FOSC is the President's designated on-scene representative and, as such, is responsible for coordinating effective response oper-

Two Coast Guard members examine a sample taken from an oil spill. Through forensic oil analysis, the USCG Marine Safety Laboratory can often determine who is responsible for the spill by comparing samples like these to oil samples from vessels in the area.

ations among a diverse group of government and commercial entities in emotion-charged and often dangerous emergency situations.

While the health of our Nation's waters and marine resources is vital to our economy, our waterways are also an economic highway essential to the Nation's access to several billion tons of foreign and domestic freight annually. Waterborne trade generates tens of millions of jobs and contributes hundreds of billions of dollars to the U.S. gross national product each year. The U.S. MTS and its inter-modal links support our economic prosperity, military strength, and national security. This complex system includes international and domestic passenger services, commercial and recreational fisheries, and recreational boating.

The Coast Guard carries out numerous port and waterways management tasks. We are responsible for providing a safe, efficient, and navigable waterway system to support domestic commerce, international trade, and military sealift requirements for national defense. We provide long and short-range aids to navigation; navigation schemes and standards; support for mapping and charting; tide, current, and pilotage information; vessel traffic services; domestic icebreaking to facilitate commerce; and technical assistance and advice.

A Coast Guard Aids to Navigation Team member inspects a light on top of a fixed aid for damage after a hurricane. The Coast Guard maintains over 51,000 aids—the largest aids to navigation system in the world.

USCGC Polar Sea operating in the Antarctic sea ice.

Finally, we operate the Nation's only Polar icebreakers. This enables our Service to project U.S. presence and protect national interests in the Arctic and Antarctic regions. These Polar vessels are key components in re-supplying U.S. Antarctic facilities. They support the research requirements of the National Science Foundation, and protect or advance other U.S. interests in the Polar Regions.

In summary, the Coast Guard's ability to fulfill its three broad roles—maritime safety, maritime security, and maritime stewardship—makes us truly a unique instrument of national policy and well-being. More than simply "guarding the coast," we help safeguard the global maritime commons.

Coast Guard International Engagement

People are often surprised when they find the U.S. Coast Guard performing duties in places far from the U.S. coast. But increasingly, the Coast Guard must accomplish its roles and missions through international activity. This reflects our Nation's global security interests as well as the integration of our maritime interests within the global system of trade, finance, information, law, and people. The Coast Guard offers three key advantages in international engagement:

Capabilities relevant to all coastal nations – Many of the world's navies and coast guards have a mix of military, law enforcement, resource protection, and humanitarian functions very similar to those of the Coast Guard. A common constabulary and multi-mission nature promotes instant understanding and interoperability and makes us a valued partner for many naval and maritime forces. The Coast Guard has a long history of providing training and support to maritime forces around the world. We also have strong partnerships based on common responsibilities, such as the North Pacific and North Atlantic Coast Guard Forums.

An HH-65 helicopter conducts medical evacuation training with a Japan Coast Guard patrol boat during North Pacific Coast Guard Forum (NPCGF) exercises. The NPCGF was initiated in 2000 as a venue to foster multilateral cooperation through the sharing of information and best practices. Current membership includes agencies from Canada, China, Japan, Korea, Russia, and the United States.

Experience in whole-of-government solutions – Building effective maritime governance requires engagement beyond navies and coast guards. It requires integrated efforts across agencies and ministries, as well as private sector commitment. The Coast Guard has this expertise by virtue of its broad statutory missions, authorities, and civil responsibilities; membership in the intelligence community; and strong partnerships with industry. We routinely engage other nations through multiple ministries and can offer a model maritime code that countries can use to improve their laws and regulations. We also find common purpose in multi-national forums and institutions, such as the International Maritime Organization, where we help advance global standards for shipping, waterways, and port facilities.

Acceptable Presence – Because of the Coast Guard's unique character, many countries routinely accept or request Coast Guard presence for promoting maritime safety, security, and stewardship, and developing local capabilities. Our blend of military and civil duties allow us to interact at exactly the level requested. Our humanitarian reputation makes our presence welcome in many regions and circumstances. This character of the Coast Guard reflects over two centuries of maritime service, and is sustained today through the enduring multi-mission professionalism and core values of Coast Guard men and women.

A U.S. Coast Guard Tactical Law Enforcement Team member demonstrates handcuff procedures during 'compliant boarding' training for service members from Dominican Republic Defence Forces at Royal Bahamas Defence Force Base Coral Harbour.

Coast Guard Forces

The Coast Guard's roles and missions are accomplished by its forces. Coast Guard forces have evolved as we have grown and today reflect the uniqueness of our Service.

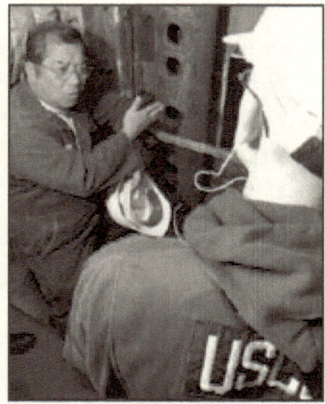

A civilian Coast Guard Marine Inspection Supervisor teaches an active duty marine inspector how to properly inspect a boiler onboard a steam-propelled passenger vessel in New York Harbor.

A reservist from Coast Guard Port Security Unit (PSU) 307 keeps a lookout for possible threats on the water in Kuwait. Coast Guard PSUs are comprised mostly of reservists and are often deployed overseas to protect strategic ports used by the U.S. Navy and coalition forces.

Workforce

Mission success is made possible by the combined activities of Coast Guard operational and support personnel. This teamwork is key to ensuring Coast Guard readiness, agility, and operational excellence. We cannot succeed without the skilled contributions, direct and indirect, of our active duty and civilian full-time employees, part-time reservists, and auxiliary volunteers. When appropriate or necessary, we also rely on the help of our many federal, state, local, tribal, and private sector partners.

The Coast Guard's full-time workforce is made up of approximately 40,000 active duty military personnel and over 7,000 civilian employees.[3] They are augmented when necessary by small numbers of civilians working under contract. This entire workforce could fit into an average size major league baseball stadium.

The Coast Guard Reserve offers citizens the opportunity to serve in the military part-time while maintaining a separate civilian career. The Reserve provides the Coast Guard highly trained and well qualified personnel for active duty in time of war and national emergency, and for augmentation of Coast Guard forces during natural or man-made disasters or accidents. The Coast Guard Reserve, numbering over 10,000 members,[4] provides the Coast Guard surge capacity and flexibility to respond to all threats and all hazards.

Nearly 30,000 strong,[5] the men and women of the uniformed all-volunteer U.S. Coast Guard Auxiliary spend thousands of hours each year, often on their personal vessels and aircraft, helping to carry out Coast Guard missions. On some waterways, Auxiliarists are the principal Coast Guard personnel serving the public. They are probably best known for their boating safety classes and courtesy vessel safety checks. However, since 1997 they have supported all Coast Guard missions except those involving military operations or law enforcement. The Coast Guard Auxiliary is the only all-volunteer component within the Department of Homeland Security.

Coast Guard Auxiliary members assist with search and rescue flight operations.

All together, this small service with a very big job numbers only about 87,000 personnel. By comparison, the next smallest U.S. armed force is the Marine Corps with over 198,000 active duty members alone.[6]

Operational Force Structure

To understand our operational structure today, it is helpful to categorize Coast Guard field operational units according to three types of forces. These are:

Multi-Mission Shore-Based Forces

Coast Guard Sector commands focus service delivery on major port regions within the U.S. and its territories. Sector commands are a consolidation of Coast Guard shore-based field operational units. These include boat stations, aids to navigation teams, and prevention and response forces such as vessel inspectors, port operations forces, communications centers, and mission controllers.

The Essential Nature of Support to Coast Guard Operations

Mission success requires the performance and devotion to duty of all Coast Guard men and women. Support personnel are as critical to mission success as those sailing cutters, flying aircraft, boarding vessels, inspecting facilities, or any other operational activity.

Support functions include:
- Human Resources (including training)
- Intelligence
- Engineering and Logistics
- Planning and Policy
- Command, Control, Communications, Computers, and Information Technology
- Capabilities Development
- Finance
- Acquisitions

Sector Commanders possess specific legal authorities for statutorily defined areas. The most important of these are:

- Captain of the Port (COTP), with authority over maritime commerce;

- Federal Maritime Security Coordinator (FMSC), with authority over maritime security;

- Officer in Charge of Marine Inspection (OCMI), with authority over vessel standards compliance;

- Search and Rescue Mission Coordinator (SMC), with authority over rescue operations; and

- Federal On-Scene Coordinator (FOSC), with authority over oil and hazardous material spill response and preparedness.

Coast Guard Sector commands are the principal enforcers of ports, waterways, and coastal laws and regulations. As such, they are the Coast Guard's key operational link to federal, state, local, tribal, and private sector partners.

A search and rescue crew from St. Louis pulls their boat down a New Orleans street looking for people in distress after Hurricane Katrina. Coast Guard Sector personnel carry out many diverse missions in coastal and inland waters.

Maritime Patrol and Interdiction Forces

Coast Guard cutters, aircraft, and their crews make up the second type of forces. These multi-mission platforms are assigned operations domestically or globally, and enable maritime presence, patrol, response, and interdiction throughout the maritime domain. With their military command, control, and communications networks, they allow the Coast Guard to deter criminal activity and respond to threats and natural or man-made emergencies.

The National Security Cutter *Bertholf* and an HC-144A Ocean Sentry maritime patrol aircraft operate in the Gulf of Mexico.

The Coast Guard can also provide these uniquely capable forces to the Department of Defense for national security contingencies. Our newest cutters and aircraft are highly adaptable and capable of meeting current and future homeland and national security needs around the world. Networked and mobile, our cutters and aircraft provide domain awareness and coordinate multi-mission, inter-agency operations.

Although maritime patrol and interdiction forces work principally in the offshore and international environments, they can also operate near shore or within ports. This is critical following a disaster or major disruption to local command, control, and communications capabilities. As the Nation's only provider of Polar icebreaking capabilities, the Coast Guard enables unique access and capabilities in the Polar Regions.

Deployable Specialized Forces

Deployable Specialized Forces (DSFs) are rapidly transportable elements with specialized skills in law enforcement, military port security, hazardous spill response, and other such missions. These specialized teams provide the Coast Guard with surge capability

and flexibility. The Deployable Operations Group (DOG) oversees, coordinates, and integrates Coast Guard DSFs, which include some reserve-based units. The DOG also works with other DHS components and government agencies to develop integrated, multi-agency, force packages to address maritime threats and hazards.

Members of the Coast Guard Deployable Operations Group practice fast-roping during a training exercise.

Forces within the DOG include:

- Maritime Safety and Security Teams (MSSTs), which include security and boat forces;
- Maritime Security Response Team (MSRT), which has specialized capabilities for law enforcement;
- Tactical Law Enforcement Teams (TACLETs) and Law Enforcement Detachments (LEDETs), which deploy wherever needed for law enforcement missions;
- Port Security Units (PSUs), which provide expeditionary port security; and
- National Strike Force (NSF), which provides high-end pollution and hazardous material response.

The U.S. Coast Guard of today is the result of the combination of five previously independent federal agencies. They are, clockwise from top:

U.S. Revenue Cutter Service ('The Defeat of the Privateer Dart,' painting by Dean Ellis);
Steamboat Inspection Service (19th century engraving of a steamboat);
U.S. Life-Saving Service ('Pea Island Lifesaving Crew Makes A Rescue,' painting by Roy la Grone);
Bureau of Navigation (Pilot's Certificate of Inspection dated June 26, 1889); and,
U.S. Lighthouse Service ('Lighthouse Ruf Stuff,' painting by John Wisinski).

Chapter Two

An Evolving Coast Guard

*T*he Coast Guard's evolution parallels that of the United States, which is a coastal nation heavily dependent upon the seas surrounding it for commerce, resources, and a buffer against external threats. The predecessor agencies of the Coast Guard were created in response to threats that arose to our Nation's vital interests as the Nation grew. As those threats evolved, so did the agencies' duties and their relationships with each other. The eventual result was consolidation, beginning in 1915 with the merging of the Revenue Cutter Service and Life-Saving Service, to form the U.S. Coast Guard. By 1946, the Coast Guard had assimilated other agencies as well.

Since that time, the Service has been assigned additional statutory responsibilities. The result is that today's Coast Guard, which carries out civil and military duties touching virtually every facet of the maritime environment, bears little resemblance to its collection of various predecessors. Yet the process of integrating these agencies, each with its own culture and characteristics, has shaped the Coast Guard in lasting ways. Understanding the evolutionary process that led to the modern Coast Guard thus provides insight into the unique nature of our Service, and the principles of Coast Guard operations that flow from it.

Coast Guard history can be divided into seven distinct periods. Our ability to uphold and protect the Nation's enduring maritime interests expanded—though not always evenly—during each of these eras.

Periods in Coast Guard History

- **1790-1865: Revenue Protection and More**
- **1866-1914: Expanding Duties for a Growing Nation**
- **1915-1916: Establishment of the U.S. Coast Guard**
- **1917-1946: A Service Forged by War, Crisis, and Consolidation**
- **1947-1972: Sorting Out Roles and Missions**
- **1973-2001: A Unique Instrument of National Security**
- **September 11, 2001, and Beyond: America's Maritime Guardian**

1790 to 1865: Revenue Protection and More

The founding of the Revenue Marine was stimulated by the financial needs of a new nation. After the Revolution, the United States was deep in debt, and its emerging industries were under tremendous pressure from British imports. The American merchant marine, a mainstay of the colonial economy, had been weakened by losses in the war. To secure its political independence, the United States first had to secure its financial independence. To accomplish this imperative, Alexander Hamilton, the first Secretary of the Treasury, proposed a bold economic plan, relying heavily on income generated by customs duties and tonnage taxes that discriminated against foreign goods and ships.

Hamilton understood that in order for his plan to succeed "the Treasury needed a strong right arm"[7] to suppress smuggling

Alexander Hamilton

and ensure duties and taxes were paid. He thus sought authorization from Congress to build "so many boats or cutters, not exceeding ten, as may be employed for the protection of revenue."[8] Enacted on August 4, the Tariff Act of 1790 authorized the building of ten cutters, but did not define their exact specifications. Most were "Baltimore Clipper" type two-masted schooners that were "light, fast, easily managed, seaworthy vessels, handy in beating in and out of harbors and through winding river channels."[9] The Tariff Act also authorized a corps of 80 men and 20 boys—the Revenue Marine—charged with a single purpose: assistance in the collection of customs duties and tonnage taxes.[10]

Hamilton also understood that for the new nation to earn customs duties and tonnage taxes, ships had to make it safely to port. Essential to that end were lighthouses, of which there were twelve in 1789, each erected and maintained by local interests.[11] Hamilton realized lighthouses were of national value; therefore, he proposed to Congress that responsibility for all aids to navigation be given to the central government.

Congress agreed, and on August 7, 1789, the Treasury Department was given responsibility for constructing and maintaining all of the Nation's aids to navigation.[12] In just its Ninth Act, the First Congress thus accepted safety of life at sea as a public responsibility and "launched the national government upon its course of guarding the coast in the interest of safety and security afloat."[13]

Boston Light is the sight of America's first lighthouse, built in 1716. The first light was burned by retreating British forces during the Revolution. This is the second tower, built in 1783 and modified in 1859.

Revenue Cutters for National Defense

For nearly seven years, Revenue Marine cutters were the only armed ships the United States possessed, the Navy having been disbanded after the Revolution. Consequently, when the Quasi-War with France loomed in 1797, the Revenue Marine was available for duty and Congress assigned the Service its first military tasks. In the same act that established the United States Navy, Congress authorized the President to augment the Navy with revenue cutters when needed.[14] Eight revenue cutters were subsequently deployed under Navy control along the U.S. southern coast and in the Caribbean from 1798 to 1799. These cutters performed national defense duties and preyed upon French shipping. At the conflict's conclusion, the Navy retained three cutters and returned five to the Revenue Marine.

For the most part, the Navy considered the cutters too small and slow for strictly naval duties.[15] Nevertheless, the need for sufficient numbers and types of warships led to the Revenue Marine's participation in naval operations on many other occasions. With only

The revenue cutter *Eagle* engages the French privateer *Bon Pere* in 1799 during the Quasi-War with France.

six frigates in service, the Navy needed the services of more armed vessels as the Nation entered the War of 1812. Revenue cutters again were absorbed into Navy service, and one promptly captured the first British prize of the war.

Shallow-draft revenue cutters proved useful in the small conflicts that erupted along the North American coastline as the Nation expanded. From 1836 to 1839, cutters engaged in littoral and riverine operations during the Seminole War in Florida. Revenue Marine vessels also participated in amphibious operations during the Mexican War in 1846–1848.

As the Nation and the U.S. Navy grew, the small numbers of armed vessels the Revenue Marine could contribute to national defense duties became relatively less important. However, the Service remained a repository for militarily useful, shallow-draft warships that were always in demand for littoral operations, and revenue cutter officers and crews who performed many gallant actions in support of the Navy.

Supporting Maritime Trade

From its earliest days, Revenue Marine efforts were not focused solely on customs collections. Instead, the Service adopted a wider role of protecting and fostering—as well as regulating—marine transportation and trade. During the presidencies of George Washington and John Adams, the Revenue Marine began maintaining aids to navigation, assisting lighthouse personnel, and charting coastal waters. It also carried out various health and quarantine measures at major ports. On the law enforcement side, beginning in 1819, the Revenue Marine worked with the Navy to drive pirates out of the coastal waters of the southern Atlantic and Gulf of Mexico, clearing those areas of threats to traders.

The Service also took on the major task of finding and rescuing distressed mariners, something it had done hitherto on an ad hoc basis. In 1832, Treasury Secretary Louis McLane ordered Revenue Marine cutters to begin limited cruising during the winter months to assist mariners in distress. This experiment was so successful that in 1837 Congress authorized the President "to cause any suitable number of public vessels…to cruise upon the coast, in the severe portion of the season…to afford such aid to distressed navigators as their circumstances and necessities may require."[16] Thus began a tradition of assistance to life and property that today is one of the Coast Guard's most widely appreciated missions.

During this same period, steamboats were plying the Nation's rivers and beginning to venture out to sea, but their boilers were notoriously unreliable and dangerous. In 1832, explosions destroyed 14 percent of all steamers in operation, with the loss of a thousand or more lives. The situation cried out for action, and in 1838 Congress enacted the first navigation law for "better securing the lives…on board vessels propelled in whole or in part by steam."[17] This Act, which gave U.S. district judges authority to appoint steamboat inspectors, is considered the beginning of an organization that would evolve over the next several decades into the Steamboat Inspection Service

Sculptured relief on the U.S. Department of Commerce headquarters building. Steamboat inspection was the precursor to the Coast Guard's marine inspection programs of today.

within the Treasury Department. It also launched what has become "an enduring national policy of regulating private enterprise in the interest of safety afloat."[18]

Almost ten years later, Congressman William Newell of New Jersey, who years earlier had personally witnessed the grounding of the bark *Terasco* and the death of the crew, set in motion a series of legislative moves that led to the formation of the U.S. Life-Saving Service. The Life-Saving Service and the Revenue Marine worked together closely—Revenue Marine personnel often were temporarily assigned to the Life-Saving Service, and cutters provided material support to lifeboat stations along the U.S. coast.

Law Enforcement in a Restive Nation

The Revenue Marine aided the federal government in enforcing its sovereignty over U.S. affairs, but its actions were not always popular in a country that was still searching for a balance between central and state power. Congress passed the Embargo and Non-Intercourse Acts in 1807 and 1809, respectively, in an attempt to keep the United States neutral during the Napoleonic Wars. Both the Revenue Marine and the Navy were called upon to prevent banned trade—an uncomfortable policy that hurt large numbers of traders, shipping companies, fishermen, and coastal communities.[19]

Beginning in 1820, the Revenue Marine also began enforcing the laws against the importation of slaves, another duty that was not universally approved of. Revenue cutters captured a number of slave ships, but it was an exercise in frustration because captured slavers were rarely prosecuted. Despite the efforts of the Revenue Marine, the U.S. Navy, and later the Royal Navy, the slave trade continued until the early 1860s.[20]

In 1832, the Revenue Marine was thrust into the national limelight when South Carolina challenged federal authority by refusing to recognize U.S. tariff laws. President Andrew Jackson sent five cutters to Charleston "to take possession of any vessel arriving from a foreign port, and defend her against any attempts to dispossess the Customs Officers of her custody."[21] Due to its link to ocean trade and the revenue that it brought the U.S. Treasury, the Revenue Marine again became part of the federal government's "long arm"—a role it would reprise 29 years later as the country headed into civil war.

Revenue Cutters in the War Between the States

As war loomed after South Carolina passed its Ordinance of Secession in December 1860, the men and cutters of the Revenue Marine faced the same dilemma as their compatriots in the Army and Navy. "Each man in federal uniform was forced to decide, and to decide quickly, whether his supreme allegiance lay with a state or with the nation-state."[22] Men chose sides, and the Revenue Marine lost men and cutters as a result.

Many, but not all, of those who remained were ordered by President Abraham Lincoln to combat service with the Navy.[23] The cutter *Harriet Lane*, which took part in the abortive relief expedition to Fort Sumter in 1861, is credited with firing the first naval shots of the Civil War.[24] Other cutters in service with the Navy performed blockade duty along the Atlantic coast, Chesapeake Bay, and Potomac River. Cutters not assigned to the Navy patrolled the shipping lanes to safeguard U.S. trade from Southern privateers and to assist distressed vessels at sea. Simultaneously, their usual duty of protecting the Nation's customs revenue took on an added urgency, since that income was critical to the Union war effort.

The revenue cutter *Harriet Lane* fires across the bow of the merchant ship *Nashville* as she enters the harbor at Charleston, South Carolina, in 1861 at the outbreak of the Civil War.

1866 to 1914: Expanding Duties for a Growing Nation

In the aftermath of the Civil War, the Nation's continuing territorial growth and the ongoing expansion of its overseas trade highlighted the need for a more effective and efficient Revenue Marine and Life-Saving Service. Reforms that began in the late 1860s ultimately improved the ability of the organizations to serve the Nation, and laid the groundwork for the formation of the modern Coast Guard.

Sumner Kimball and Service Reform

In 1869, George Boutwell, Secretary of the Treasury under President Ulysses S. Grant, formed an interim Revenue Marine Bureau under the leadership of N. Broughton Devereux. Devereux, in turn, established boards designed to overhaul and reorganize the Revenue Cutter Service, as it was now known.[25] The Revenue Marine Bureau became a permanent agency in 1871 under Treasury official Sumner I. Kimball.

Sumner I. Kimball

Kimball immediately set out to increase the professionalism of the Revenue Cutter Service. Six months after taking office, he issued revised Revenue Cutter Service regulations that provided for economy of operations, centralized control of the Service at headquarters, and officer accessions and promotions based on merit rather than political influence or seniority. Meanwhile, Bureau Chief Devereux's personnel board, headed by Captain John Faunce, USRCS, reviewed the qualifications of every Revenue Cutter Service officer and removed those found incompetent or otherwise unfit for duty. Officers retained were given rank commensurate with their capabilities, and were thereafter promoted based on the results they achieved on the professional examinations mandated in Kimball's regulations. As a result, by 1872 Kimball could proclaim his junior officer corps the best the Revenue Cutter Service had ever possessed.[26] To ensure a continuous supply of competent junior officers, Kimball persuaded Congress in 1876 to authorize establishment of a training school, thus laying the foundation for the U.S. Coast Guard Academy.[27]

Kimball and his staff also implemented the recommendations of Devereux's other board, which had analyzed the structure of the cutter fleet. Kimball reduced fleet tonnage by replacing large, aging cutters with smaller, speedier, and more efficient ones sized according to the needs of the ports where they were to be stationed. He also steadily replaced sailing ships with steamers. As a result, while from 1872 to 1881 the fleet size increased by just one cutter, 60 percent of the vessels had been built since 1869, and the ratio of steamers to sailing cutters had risen from 2.5:1 to nearly 8:1.[28] Thanks to the reforms of Kimball, Devereux, and Faunce, the Revenue Cutter Service now boasted a highly professional corps manning modern cutters well suited to their missions.

Upon appointment as chief of the Revenue Cutter Service, Kimball also instituted a program of inspecting the lifesaving stations in New Jersey and Long Island, New York, where he discovered appalling conditions. As a result of his findings, Congress appropriated funds to establish the Life-Saving Service as a branch under the supervision of the Revenue Cutter Service, to build lifesaving stations in states along the coast without one, and to staff the stations with paid surfmen. Kimball reorganized the Revenue Cutter Service to accommodate the Life-Saving Service, and applied his considerable talents to systematically improving readiness, training, personnel, and equipment standards. During this period, the Life-Saving Service also expanded its reach to cover the Gulf of Mexico, Great Lakes, and Pacific coast of the United States.[29]

> ### The Lifesaving Medals
>
> When Congress passed the Life-Saving Act of 1874, it established First and Second Class Medals to recognize daring and heroic rescues on U.S. waters. The medals were renamed Gold and Silver Lifesaving Medals in 1882.
>
> The Gold Lifesaving Medal is awarded for demonstrating extreme and heroic daring during a rescue or attempted rescue at risk of one's own life.
>
> The Silver Lifesaving Medal is awarded for extraordinary effort that does not reach the criteria for the Gold Lifesaving Medal.

Despite Kimball's effort to inculcate discipline and professionalism, the Life-Saving Service was plagued by claims that unqualified lifesavers were given their jobs solely for reasons of politics and patronage. Compounding the situation were several high profile tragedies, chief among them the losses of the *USS Huron* in November 1877, and the steamer *Metropolis* in January 1878, which produced a tremendous outcry against the Life-Saving Service. Recognizing the need to improve rescue operations, Congress passed legislation on June 18, 1878, authorizing the construction of a number of additional lifesaving stations, removing the Life-Saving Service from the Revenue Cutter Service, and appointing Sumner Kimball general superintendent of the new Service.[30] Kimball steadily eliminated the system of political patronage that had grown with the Life-Saving Service, replacing it with one based upon technical competence and nonpartisanship. However, coordination with the Revenue Cutter Service remained in force, since Revenue Cutter Service officers continued to serve as inspectors and auditors for the lifesavers.

Growing Civil Duties

Meanwhile, the United States had purchased the territory of Alaska in 1867, giving the Revenue Cutter Service a new set of sovereignty and resource protection responsibilities. In addition to increased law enforcement obligations, the Revenue Cutter Service performed many civil and humanitarian duties, mounted scientific expeditions, and protected fish and game. It was entrusted by the Bureau of Education to deliver teachers to the native communities. In fact,

Crewmen from the revenue cutter *Bear* haul supplies to whaling vessels trapped in the ice near Point Barrow, Alaska, in 1888.

so instrumental was the Revenue Cutter Service in establishing the authority of the federal government in Alaska that one could say that for many years the Revenue Cutter Service was the government along Alaska's western coast.

With the growth of the American merchant marine, the marine safety and waterways management work of the revenue cutters—supporting marine transportation and trade—also expanded.

Although they acted without a clear statutory mandate, cutter crews had long performed many tasks related to the safety of harbors and cruising grounds. In 1889, Congress passed laws to regulate anchorages, giving the Revenue Cutter Service the duty of enforcing these new laws. In 1906, lawmakers authorized the Service to clear derelict hulks from harbors and their approaches. And in 1910, the Service gained authority over some aspects of pleasure boating.

The mission of safety at sea became important internationally with the sinking of the *Titanic* in 1912, and the loss of more than 1,500 lives. This tragic event led the Revenue Cutter Service to assume ice patrol duties the following year when the Navy, which originally had assigned two cruisers to perform that mission, announced it needed the warships elsewhere. Private shipping and port organizations petitioned the Treasury Department to assign revenue cutters to what they considered an extremely valuable effort. The department granted its permission, and two cutters undertook the mission. The assumption of this seemingly natural function in the North Atlantic reflected long-standing Revenue Cutter Service practice in the Bering Sea. These ice patrols have now protected northern shipping for nearly a century without incident.

The last half of the nineteenth century also saw the Revenue Cutter Service expand its mission of protecting marine resources. Revenue Cutter Service personnel patrolled the Pribilof Islands off Alaska to prevent the ongoing slaughter of seals. The Service also worked with the Bureau of Fisheries to encourage proliferation of "food fishes" and regulated the harvesting and sale of sponges in the Gulf of Mexico.

Spanish-American War

By 1898, both the Navy and the Revenue Cutter Service were more modern, professional organizations than they had been on the eve of the U.S. Civil War. Reflecting this state of affairs, transfer of the revenue cutters to Navy control during the Spanish-American War went relatively smoothly.

For three years prior to the outbreak of war, Revenue Cutter Service cutters had conducted neutrality patrols that stretched from the waters off North Carolina to the Gulf of Mexico. They seized ships suspected of violating U.S. neutrality by smuggling ammunition and other supplies to Cuban rebels.

All of this changed with the executive order directing the Revenue Cutter Service to provide cutters to the Navy. Eight cutters joined Rear Admiral William Sampson's North Atlantic Squadron on

The revenue cutter *Hudson* during a joint Navy-Revenue Cutter Service raid on Spanish gunboats in Cardenas Bay, Cuba, during the Spanish-American War in 1898.

blockade duty off Cuba. Another cutter served as an escort and dispatch boat with Commodore George Dewey's Asiatic Squadron, which defeated a Spanish naval force at Manila Bay in the Philippines. Elsewhere, 11 cutters served under the Army's tactical control, guarding important U.S. ports on the east and west coasts against possible attacks by Spanish raiders or warships.[31]

Once again, the Revenue Cutter Service provided important inshore support to the Navy. For instance, at the specific request of President William McKinley, Congress awarded specially minted medals to the officers and the crew of the cutter Hudson (including the War's only gold medal to the captain, Lieutenant Frank H. Newcomb), recognizing their bravery under fire during a combined Navy and Revenue Cutter Service raid on Spanish gunboats in Cardenas Bay, Cuba.[32]

1915 to 1916: Establishment of the U.S. Coast Guard

The process that resulted in the formation of the U.S. Coast Guard actually began with an attempt to abolish the Revenue Cutter Service. In 1911, President William Taft appointed his economic adviser, Frederick A. Cleveland, to lead a commission to recommend ways to increase the economy and efficiency of government. The Cleveland Commission concluded that uni-functional agencies were more efficient and economical than multifunctional ones. The commission thus recommended combining the Lighthouse Service and Life-Saving Service, with their similar "protection" function, and recommended apportioning the duties and assets of the multi-functional Revenue Cutter Service among other government agencies and departments. In particular, larger cutters and their crews would be transferred to the Navy.

The Treasury, Navy, and Commerce and Labor Departments were asked to comment on the report. Secretary of Commerce and Labor Charles Nagel agreed other departments could perform many Revenue Cutter Service duties, but none could perform its lifesaving mission. This mission probably could be accomplished best, he wrote presciently, by combining the Revenue Cutter Service, the Life-Saving Service, and the Lighthouse Service. While not sure where this new combined service organization should reside within the government, Nagel was adamant that it should not be in the Navy Department.

For its part, the Navy Department stated that it could use the Revenue Cutter Service cutters, because it was short of smaller, shallow-draft ships. But Secretary of the Navy George Meyer did not relish absorbing Revenue Cutter Service personnel into the Navy. Moreover, he wrote:

> It is true that the chief functions of the Revenue Cutter Service can be performed by the Navy, but this cannot be done as stated in the Cleveland report in the regular performance of their military duties. All duties which interfere with the training of personnel for war are irregular and in a degree detrimental to the efficiency of the fleet.[33]

The final responses came from Secretary of the Treasury Franklin MacVeagh and Revenue Cutter Service Captain-Commandant Ellsworth Price Bertholf. MacVeagh in particular was defiant in defense of the Service. He pointed to the close and successful working relationship the Revenue Cutter Service and the Life-Saving Service had developed. This connection that would be severed by the abolition of the Revenue Cutter Service. He also took the Cleveland Commission to task over the alleged "efficiencies" that spreading Revenue Cutter Service duties across the government would generate. Finally, he echoed the Navy's argument concerning the nature of Revenue Cutter Service and Navy duties, stating:

[The Navy] could never give the kind and degree of attention that is required of the Revenue Cutter Service and its officers and men in their particular duties for 120 years. The [RCS's] work is alien to the work of the Navy, alien to the spirit of the Navy, and alien, I think, to its professional capacities and instincts—alien certainly to its training and tastes.[34]

Nevertheless, in April 1912, President Taft sent the Cleveland Commission's final draft and the other comments to Congress, with his recommendation that the legislators adopt the commission's findings. Revenue Cutter Service supporters within the federal government, the press, and the general public fought the move, citing in particular the Service's heroic rescue work as a reason not to disband the agency.

Meanwhile, Secretary MacVeagh ordered Bertholf and Sumner Kimball, head of the Life-Saving Service, to draft legislation that would join the Revenue Cutter Service and Life-Saving Service in a new organization. When Taft and MacVeagh left office after the 1912 election, President Woodrow Wilson and his Treasury Secretary, William Gibbs McAdoo, strongly supported the bill combining the two services. The Senate passed the bill in 1914 and the House passed it in early 1915, after a debate that centered more upon cutter officer and surfman pay and retirement benefits than conceptual issues.

Ellsworth Price Bertholf

There will not be two services. There will not be a Life-Saving Service and a Revenue Cutter Service. It will be the coast guard.

— Captain-Commandant Ellsworth Price Bertholf, testifying on combining the RCS and LSS, 1915

Combining the civilian Life-Saving Service and the military Revenue Cutter Service—organizations with vastly different cultures—into a single military service, presented a delicate challenge to Captain Bertholf, who was named the first Coast Guard Commandant. Bertholf was absolutely convinced that the military character of the Revenue Cutter Service had to prevail, but large numbers of the lifesavers had no desire to change their civilian status. Consequently, while the Life-

Saving Service and Revenue Cutter Service were joined at the top in 1915, they operated as separate entities within the Coast Guard for more than 15 years. However, events soon would accelerate the development of a twentieth-century maritime security force formed by the union of these two nineteenth-century institutions.

1917 to 1946: A Service Forged by War, Crisis, and Consolidation

Only two years after its formation, the Coast Guard was plunged into war. World War I was the first in a series of events that would shape the Service during the next several decades, and expand its maritime duties. Some of these events, such as Prohibition and World War II, significantly increased the size of the Coast Guard.

The Coast Guard in The Great War

World War I saw the Coast Guard transferred to the Navy to fight overseas. In previous wars, Revenue Cutter Service cutters had served under Navy control, but the Revenue Cutter Service itself had remained under the Treasury Department. During The Great War, however, the entire Service was transferred to Navy control as prescribed in the act that created the Coast Guard.

In the period leading up to America's entry into the war, the Coast Guard and Navy began rudimentary planning for integrating the Coast Guard into naval operations—a first in the history of both services. For the most part, the Navy believed that Coast Guard forces would be best suited for coastal patrol, although a few of the larger cutters were designated for convoy escort operations. The services did not develop any detailed plans, but Coast Guard units did participate in some naval preparedness drills.

The Coast Guard was actually mobilized and transferred to the Navy in April 1917. The Service sent six cutters to European waters that summer. For the remainder of the war, the cutters escorted convoys between Gibraltar and the British Isles. They also performed escort and patrol duties in the Mediterranean.

At home, one of the Coast Guard's major tasks was port security. Concern over the possibility of accidents and sabotage was acute in the aftermath of an October 1917 shipboard explosion in the port of Halifax, Nova Scotia. In that incident, a French steamer loaded with ammunition collided with another vessel and caught fire. The resulting explosion leveled a large portion of the town, and caused more than 1,000 civilian deaths and numerous other casualties. U.S. ports handled more wartime shipping than Halifax, making the issue of port security even more pressing. As a

result, the Treasury Department, working closely with the Navy, established Coast Guard Captain of the Port offices in New York, Philadelphia, Norfolk, and Sault Ste. Marie. The New York office soon became the Coast Guard's largest command.

The *USCGC Tampa*, which was sunk by a German torpedo in September 1918 with 131 crewmen aboard.

Thus, the Coast Guard's role of ensuring maritime mobility in U.S. ports and waterways expanded considerably. Along the remainder of the U.S. coast, lifesaving station personnel doubled as coast-watchers, maintaining a lookout for potential infiltrators. To facilitate the reporting of suspicious activity, many lifesaving stations were tied into the Navy's communication system, which ultimately improved the Coast Guard's peacetime communications as well.

Interdiction and Buildup

When the war ended in November 1918, cutters gradually began to return from overseas service, but the Coast Guard did not pass immediately back to Treasury Department control. A new political storm brewed as proponents of the Navy (including Navy Secretary Josephus Daniels), Congress, and even Coast Guard officers from the old Revenue Cutter Service, struggled to keep the Service permanently under the Navy Department. The Navy was determined to retain control of all government vessels, and most Coast Guard officers did not wish to relinquish the more generous pay, promotion, and social benefits that accrued to Navy officers. But in 1919—after strong protests and canny advocacy by Captain-Commandant

Bertholf and Treasury Secretary Carter Glass—the Service was returned to the Treasury Department.

Still, the period immediately following World War I was the most difficult the Coast Guard ever faced, and within just a few years, the Service would experience its greatest peacetime growth. The catalyst for this expansion was the 1919 National Prohibition (Volstead) Act, which prohibited the manufacture, sale, and transportation of alcoholic beverages within the United States. With no other federal agency prepared to enforce the new law at sea, much of the burden of enforcing the Volstead Act fell to the Coast Guard.

The Coast Guard began its enforcement effort with just over 100 vessels to cover vast distances along the shores of the Atlantic, Pacific, Great Lakes, and Gulf States. This situation created several years of relative ineffectiveness. Beginning in 1924, however, Congress appropriated funds sufficient to allow the Service to begin a major expansion to meet its responsibilities under the law. Over the next ten years, the Coast Guard budget increased dramatically and the Service grew accordingly. The enlisted force tripled in size, as did the fleet. The Service acquired and refurbished 31 obsolete Navy destroyers for use in picketing the foreign supply ships that lay offshore, outside U.S. territorial waters. A large force of specially designed Coast Guard patrol boats and harbor craft, plus a number of seized smuggling vessels, patrolled inshore waters and pursued the rumrunner contact boats. When even this proved insufficient, the Coast Guard began using aircraft to report suspicious vessels. This action marked the birth of Coast Guard aviation.[35]

While this initial buildup, and a decade-long effort, did have a deterrent effect on the rumrunners, the interdiction effort ultimately failed because the law was unpopular, and the demand for alcohol never ceased. In 1933, the 21st Amendment to the U.S. Constitution finally repealed the 18th Amendment and with it Prohibition. Still, the Coast Guard benefited from its Prohibition experience. Patrol boats built during this period conducted numerous missions for many decades and served as prototypes for later vessel classes. Coast Guard communications equipment, procedures, and intelligence methods were significantly improved. Tactics and techniques developed to combat the rumrunners would be used decades later to combat drug smugglers. And the Service developed international law expertise through its efforts to increase the limit of the territorial sea from three to 12 nautical miles.

The Waesche Consolidation

After Prohibition, Admiral Russell R. Waesche, Sr., Coast Guard Commandant from 1936 to 1945, guided one of the greatest transitions in the Service's history. In many ways, his vision was responsible for today's Coast Guard. Waesche oversaw the addition of many responsibilities, the most sweeping of which was Congressional authorization for the Coast Guard to enforce all U.S. laws at sea and within territorial waters.

Russell R. Waesche, Sr.

Hitherto, most observers had assumed the Coast Guard had broad law enforcement authority at sea. However, a 1927 Supreme Court case had called that authority into question. At the Treasury Department's request, Congress clarified the situation in 1936, granting Coast Guard personnel the authority to make "inquiries, examinations, inspections, searches, seizures, and arrests upon the high seas and the navigable waters of the United States."[36] The Service was also tasked to break ice in the Nation's harbors and channels, and took on a small role in the certification of merchant seamen. That role expanded in 1938 to include administration of the U.S. Maritime Service, formed that year to improve the efficiency of merchant mariners.

Waesche also saw the need to regulate boating activity in the Nation's waters. Lacking the manpower to perform this function, in 1939 he created the civilian uniformed volunteer force now called the Coast Guard Auxiliary to meet this specific need. By 1940, the Auxiliary had 2,600 personnel and 2,300 boats that augmented the Coast Guard at a fraction of the cost of a full-time force. Waesche's greatest force multiplier, however, was the military Coast Guard Reserve, created in 1941. This gave the Coast Guard the potential to perform many roles and missions that would otherwise be impossible for a small service.[37]

Also in 1939, as part of President Franklin Roosevelt's reorganization plans, the U.S. Lighthouse Service was placed under the Coast Guard. Waesche welcomed this addition, recognizing that it gave the Coast Guard an all-encompassing role in ensuring the safety of the Nation's waterways. Absorbing the Lighthouse Service also added nearly 50 percent more civilians to the Service, caused a district reorganization, and brought many of the lighthouse personnel into the Service's military ranks.

Additional responsibilities continued to accrue throughout Waesche's tenure. In 1940, for example, the Coast Guard was tasked with open-ocean weather patrol duties in the North Atlantic (and later northern Pacific Ocean), a service it would continue to perform for nearly 40 years.

National Defense to the Fore

With the outbreak of war in Europe in 1939, the Coast Guard—having had its civil responsibilities vastly increased since World War I—once again shifted focus to emphasize military preparedness and Coast Guard forces would play a major role in asserting national sovereignty over U.S. waters and shipping. The Coast Guard began carrying out neutrality patrols in the North Atlantic in September 1939, and put port security forces on a wartime footing the following June.

U.S. strategists also were concerned that Germany would establish a military presence in Greenland, which had been incorporated into the U.S. hemispheric defense system. The U.S. government sought to station military forces on that frozen island, but the State Department cautioned this would be unnecessarily provocative.[38] Eventually, however, the Coast Guard was deemed an acceptable U.S. military presence, and in April 1941, the Coast Guard took responsibility for cold weather operations in Greenland.

By Executive Order 8929 of November 1, 1941, over a month before the Japanese attack on Pearl Harbor, Hawaii, President Roosevelt transferred the Coast Guard to the Navy for the second time in its history. Thereafter, Coast Guard cutters and aircraft performed extensive convoy protection duties in the Atlantic (sinking 12 German U-boats), while other Service craft performed area antisubmarine patrols. Coast Guard craft rescued the survivors of torpedo attacks off the U.S. coast, while Coast Guard coast-watchers maintained beach patrols and guarded U.S. ports. Coast Guard personnel manned Navy destroyer escorts as well as Navy and Army amphibious ships and craft, and took part in every major amphibious invasion of the war.

Allied troops wade to shore from a Coast Guard-crewed landing craft during the Normandy invasion, June 6, 1944.

Coast Guard personnel served in theater around the globe during the war years, but the Service also made a significant contribution to the war effort in rear areas, protecting and facilitating the movement of men and materiel by sea. Coast Guard activities in the maritime mobility area—providing port security, supervising the movement of dangerous cargoes, controlling merchant vessel traffic, maintaining aids to navigation, and breaking ice—often received less public attention than its direct combat duties, but they were indispensable to prosecution of the war.[39]

World War II also gave the Coast Guard the opportunity to experiment and innovate. It was a Coast Guard officer, Lieutenant Commander Lawrence M. Harding, who guided the development of a new electronic Long-Range Aid to Navigation—LORAN—and the subsequent deployment of the LORAN network.[40]

During the war, a few farsighted officers doggedly pursued the development of helicopters for use in search and rescue, law enforcement, and antisubmarine patrol. Initially cool to the idea until he witnessed a demonstration, Admiral Waesche urged Chief of Naval Operations Admiral Ernest King to develop the helicopter for naval use. King, in turn, ordered the Coast Guard to obtain helicopters for use in antisubmarine surveillance. The Service acquired a handful of aircraft and trained Coast Guard, Navy, and British aircrews to fly them. While they never saw much success against submarines, these helicopters demonstrated an immediate usefulness in search and rescue, foreshadowing the role for which they would become famous.

An HNS-1 helicopter, piloted by a Coast Guard officer, lifts off from the converted merchant ship *Daghestan* in January 1944, while in convoy from New York to Liverpool, England.

In addition to driving mission and technological innovation, the war had a major effect on the size and shape of the Service. During the war years, the Coast Guard experienced a nearly tenfold increase in personnel strength. The Roosevelt Administration also decided it would be convenient and cost-effective to consolidate the functions of the Bureau of Marine Inspection and Navigation into the Coast Guard. The roots of this agency stretched back to 1838, when the Steamboat Inspection Service was created. In 1932, this agency had merged with the Bureau of Navigation, which had been created in 1884. Now called the Bureau of Marine Inspection and Navigation, this civilian agency joined the Coast Guard permanently in 1946. As a result, Coast Guard missions now touched every facet of domestic maritime activity. The Service's duties expanded overseas as well, as the United States took the lead in shaping the post-war world.

1947 to 1972: Sorting Out Roles and Missions

The post-World War II period brought further changes as the Coast Guard inherited new missions and once again saw its roles redefined and broadened. Perhaps foreseeing this expansion, and mindful of the growing pains the Service had suffered during the war, the farsighted Waesche created a committee in 1944 to develop a comprehensive post-war plan to retain the functions the Service had absorbed in the 1930s and 1940s.

Subsequently, the 1948 Ebasco Study determined that the Coast Guard was undermanned and under equipped to perform its many and wide-ranging missions. This led to legislation that formally delineated the Coast Guard's duties. These included port management, control, and security functions; vessel traffic services; coastal security; and some military roles.

An International Role in Peacetime and in War

After the war, the Coast Guard gained a significant global peacetime presence as part of its efforts to safeguard transoceanic navigation. The Service retained operational control over a regional wide-area system of LORAN transmitter sites. The need to support our burgeoning civil aviation system also led to Coast Guard cutters continuing to maintain a network of open ocean weather stations until 1977, by which time improvements in weather forecasting and aircraft navigation and safety had made the service unnecessary. On scene to provide weather and communications support to transatlantic and transpacific flights, cutters on ocean station duty also conducted several high profile at-sea rescues of the passengers and crews of civil and military aircraft. Perhaps the most significant of these was the rescue of all 62 passengers and seven crewmembers from the ditched flying boat *Bermuda Sky Queen* by the cutter *Bibb* operating on a mid-Atlantic ocean station. Cutters continued to conduct international ice patrols as well, although this duty eventually became the province of Coast Guard aircraft detachments.

The Coast Guard's diverse capabilities and inherent flexibility allowed the Service to support even broader American political and military policies overseas in the post-war period. For instance, the Service helped establish the Japanese Maritime Safety Agency and the navies of Korea and the Philippines. It also participated—and still does participate—in numerous military exercises with South American navies, and conducts training with small navies and coast guards around the world.

The Coast Guard participated only marginally in the Korean War. During the Vietnam War, however, the Coast Guard played a major role in "Operation Market Time," which involved the interdiction of trawlers used by North Vietnam for infiltration and re-supply activities.

Five Coast Guard 311-foot high endurance cutters, assigned to Operation Market Time in Vietnam, tied up alongside the Navy repair ship *Jason*.

Working together, the U.S. Navy and the South Vietnamese Navy (VNN) had attempted to halt the flow of enemy men and materiel, but the VNN's lack of training and the U.S. Navy's dearth of shallow-draft warships and coastal operating experience frustrated the effort. Consequently, Navy Secretary Paul Nitze wrote Treasury Secretary Henry Fowler for assistance. After noting the Seventh Fleet's deficiencies, Nitze wrote: "We are therefore attempting to locate a source of more suitable patrol craft. Such characteristics as high speed, shallow draft, sea-keeping ability, radar, and communications equipment are important considerations."[41]

Coast Guard Commandant Admiral Edwin Roland believed that Coast Guard forces were tailor-made for the mission. Moreover, he also feared that if the Coast Guard did not play a greater role than it had during the Korean War, the Service might lose its status as an armed force. Thus, after deliberations in Washington and in the field, 26 Coast Guard 82-foot patrol boats and their crews were assigned to Operation Market Time.

In March 1967, when the Navy needed additional destroyers for naval gunfire support duties, it drew down the number of its own ships conducting Market Time patrols. Secretary Nitze turned again to the Coast Guard to fill the resulting gaps in surveillance and interdiction and requested "that the Treasury Department assist the Department of the Navy by assigning five high endurance cutters to augment Market Time forces.[42] The Coast Guard responded by deploying a squadron of high endurance cutters.

Together, Coast Guard, Navy, and VNN assets formed a gauntlet through which Viet Cong supply vessels had to run to reach their objectives. Navy patrol aircraft monitored vessels more than 100 nautical miles from the coast. Navy radar picket ships and Coast Guard high endurance cutters formed a second barrier 40 nautical miles out. Coast Guard patrol boats, Navy Swift Boats, and VNN junks formed the final barrier just off the coast and up South Vietnam's rivers. By the end of Operation Market Time, the Coast Guard had boarded nearly a quarter of a million sampans and junks and destroyed more than 2,000. The maritime border of South Vietnam was sealed and eliminated as a re-supply route for communist forces.

The crew of *USCGC Point Comfort*, on duty with U.S. naval forces in Vietnam, searches a Vietnamese craft for weapons and supplies.

Expanding Civil Responsibilities

The Coast Guard's civil duties continued to expand in the period following World War II. In 1958, the Service developed AMVER, a ship reporting system able to identify other ships in the area of a vessel in distress so that assistance could be vectored to the site.[43] In 1965, the Service took responsibility for coordinating all search and rescue operations in U.S. waters, and that same year accepted responsibility for all of the Nation's icebreaking duties. Until then, both the Navy and the Coast Guard had performed icebreaking assignments. When the Navy concluded that its personnel and resources should be devoted to more traditional naval combat operations, however, it offered the mission and its five-ship icebreaking fleet to the Coast Guard. The two Services signed a memorandum of understanding, and the ships were gradually phased into the Coast Guard, which then became the primary U.S. surface presence in the Polar Regions.

Meanwhile, the Coast Guard's traditional maritime law and sovereignty enforcement role remained important. Circumstances in Cuba, for example, handed the Service a greater role in enforcing U.S. immigration policy and controlling the flow of seaborne migrants. The Coast Guard began patrols to enforce U.S. neutrality and to aid Cuban refugees in the Florida Straits in 1961. Then, in 1964, the Camarioca boatlift first tested the Service's ability to respond to a mass exodus. Repeated mass migrations from Cuba and Haiti over the next three decades would continue to hone Coast Guard capabilities in this area.

Finding a New Home

As the Nation moved further into the 20th century the Coast Guard again found itself in a familiar situation. The Service had come to perform so many types of maritime missions, in so many areas, and for so many purposes, that it did not fit perfectly in any one federal department. While the Coast Guard and most of its predecessors had been part of the Treasury Department since their founding, the traditional direct link between collecting revenue and the Service had faded.

The result was President Lyndon Johnson's decision to incorporate the Coast Guard into the newly formed Department of Transportation in April 1967. At first, Treasury Secretary Fowler and Coast Guard Commandant Roland protested, but the President and his staff had already resolved that many key Coast Guard functions belonged in the new department. Rather than see these stripped from the Service, Roland cooperated in the transfer. Nevertheless, he successfully argued that that the Coast Guard should remain a military service.[44]

1973 to 2001: A Unique Instrument of National Security

In the immediate post-Vietnam era, the United States continued to face complex and varied threats around the world. And increasingly, the Coast Guard's unique status as a military service and law enforcement agency brought it to the forefront of U.S. maritime security efforts. For instance, social upheaval in the Western Hemisphere highlighted the critical importance of the Coast Guard's undocumented migrant interdiction mission. The Service faced the challenge of mass migrations from Cuba in 1980 and 1994, and from Haiti in 1992 and 1994.

The influx of illegal drugs also came to the fore as a national security problem in the 1970s. The Coast Guard took on the primary maritime interdiction role, and eventually expanded its Caribbean presence to disrupt the illegal drug trade. The Service's efforts effectively neutralized the seaborne importation of marijuana, which slowed to a trickle after a prolonged and concerted Coast Guard effort. Unfortunately, as the marijuana trade dried up, the shipment of cocaine began to increase.

The Coast Guard's environmental protection responsibilities grew as well. While the Revenue Marine had been tasked with protecting valuable natural resources as early as 1822[45] and defending the marine environment as a whole beginning with the Refuse Act of 1899,[46] growing environmental awareness in the United States pushed the Coast Guard deeper into the antipollution realm.

The *Torrey Canyon* and *Amoco Cadiz* tanker groundings led to the Federal Water Pollution Control Act of 1972, in which Congress set a no-discharge standard for oil in U.S. navigable waters. The practice of discharging shipboard oily residues at sea led to an October 1973 convention adopted by the International Conference on Marine Pollution prohibiting oil discharges within 50 miles of shore.

Given responsibility for coordinating and administering oil spill cleanup in the maritime realm, the Coast Guard adopted a multi-faceted strategy for responding to spills and identifying responsible parties. The Service developed techniques to detect spills from the air and to match samples of spilled oil to the oil remaining in the tanks of suspected polluters. Three strike teams composed of Coast Guard personnel trained to operate special oil spill cleanup equipment were stood up, one each on the Atlantic, Pacific, and Gulf coasts. And each Captain of the Port identified a local network of contractors who could respond to spills.

Yet the spills continued. On December 15, 1976, the Liberian tanker, *Argo Merchant*, carrying 7.5 million gallons of oil, grounded off Nantucket Island, Massachusetts. While favorable winds drove the oil out to sea instead of onto the beaches of New England, this ecological near miss, together with the fourteen more tanker accidents that occurred in or near American waters during the next ten weeks, led to the Port and Tanker Safety Act of 1978. This legislation created a 200-mile pollution control zone and authorized the Coast Guard to prohibit substandard foreign tankers from calling on U.S. ports.

The *Exxon Valdez* oil tanker aground in Prince William Sound, Alaska, in 1989.

The 1989 *Exxon Valdez* oil spill in Prince William Sound, Alaska, had the greatest impact on the Coast Guard's role as protector of the marine environment. The Service would not only oversee the clean-up, but the Oil Pollution Act of 1990 (OPA 90) passed by Congress in the wake of the spill gave the Coast Guard one of its single largest legislative mandates in its history. OPA 90 assigned the Service a significantly increased role in spill response, vessel inspection, and the oversight of liability actions.

During the years following World War II, America also witnessed a number of serious hazardous material incidents. By 1973, Congress had broadened the scope of the National Contingency Plan to include the framework and regulatory requirements for responding to hazardous substance spills. This placed Coast Guard Federal On-Scene Coordinators and strike teams at the forefront of responding to all releases—not just maritime—in their areas of responsibility.

The experience gained over the next three decades established the Coast Guard as a leader in preparedness and response, and would prove instrumental in National Strike Force performance following the terrorist attacks of September 11, 2001.

Another rising environmental concern in the 1970s pertained to the perceived depredation of America's abundant fisheries resources by large foreign fishing fleets. In the 1950s, the United States had implemented several international conventions intended to protect certain fish stocks. The Coast Guard documented violations by foreign fishing vessels, but had little direct enforcement authority. Congress addressed the situation in 1964 with the Bartlett Act, which prohibited foreign fishing in U.S. territorial waters and authorized the seizure of foreign vessels in violation of the law. Later amendments expanded the protected area to include the 12-mile contiguous zone, and increased the maximum penalty for violations.

In 1976, when even these protections were deemed inadequate, Congress passed the Magnuson-Stevens Fishery Conservation and Management Act. The Act established a 200-nautical mile Exclusive Economic Zone; created eight Regional Fishery Management Councils tasked to develop management plans to protect America's fish stocks; and placed the primary responsibility for at-sea enforcement of the Nation's fisheries laws with the Coast Guard. In the ensuing decades, the Service gained authority to enforce a series of legislative enactments and international agreements intended to protect the Nation's living marine resources.

Beginning in 1984, the Service was assigned the responsibility to command Maritime Defense Zones (MDZs) to provide for the coastal defense of the United States in times of war. This was a significant shift in our national defense posture. Under the MDZ construct, Department of Defense forces would be commanded by Coast Guard flag officers if an MDZ was activated. In 1994, the MDZ concept was expanded to include defense of foreign harbors, expeditionary port security, and coastal sea control. The MDZ construct is no longer used. U.S. Northern Command has now assumed responsibility for commanding forces that may be used to defend U.S. coasts in times of war. In peace time, the security of our domestic ports and waterways remains the responsibility of the U.S. Coast Guard and other agencies working with the Port Security and Port Readiness Committees.

The Service played a role in post-Cold War military operations as well. Coast Guard PSUs were deployed to the Persian Gulf during Operations Desert Shield and Desert Storm in 1990–1991.

Coast Guard port security raider boats provide force protection for the U.S. Navy guided-missile cruiser *USS Normandy*.

At the same time, Captains of the Port ensured the safe transport of expeditionary troops and munitions by overseeing explosive loads, establishing security zones, and providing escorts. In recent years, the unified combatant commanders have requested—and been provided—cutters to conduct maritime interception operations, peacetime military engagement, and other supporting warfare tasks for deployed Navy Fleets.[47]

During Operations Support Democracy (November 1993–August 1995) and Uphold Democracy (October 1994–March 1995), Coast Guard cutters and port security units supported United Nations led operations to restore democratic institutions in Haiti. Two port security units, a harbor defense command unit, five law enforcement detachments, and 13 cutters carried out operations that included maritime surveillance and interdiction, search and rescue coverage for in-transit U.S. aircraft, and establishing and restoring aids to navigation.

September 11, 2001, and Beyond: America's Maritime Guardian

Coast Guard National Strike Force members respond to the September 11, 2001, attacks on the World Trade Center in New York.

A Dark Moment and New Chapter for the Coast Guard

In the immediate aftermath of the terrorist attacks of September 11, 2001, New York area Coast Guard personnel were among the first responders to the World Trade Center tragedy and assisted in evacuating more than half a million people by water from lower Manhattan. The Coast Guard also mobilized more than 2,700 reservists in the largest homeland defense and port security operation since World War II. These reservists, and their active duty counterparts, provided the manpower and expertise for cleanup efforts in New York City. They heightened security in ports and increased vigilance along the Nation's 95,000 miles of coastline, including the Great Lakes and inland waterways. The Coast Guard's National Strike Force was also at the forefront of a multi-agency response to anthrax cases in Washington, DC, and Florida. But even as these contingency operations gathered momentum, more far-reaching developments were already underway.

The Homeland Security Act of 2002 transferred the Coast Guard to the Department of Homeland Security as the maritime element of the Nation's new security organization. However, unlike within the Department of Defense, the Commandant, as service chief, reports directly to the Secretary. Additionally, the Coast Guard's missions and organization remained intact, despite a heightened focus on maritime homeland security. Congress decided that all of the Service's authorities and missions should remain as part of the larger total-security construct.

In Operation Iraqi Freedom in 2003, the nation again called upon the Coast Guard's expertise in maritime security and national defense. The Coast Guard deployed two high endurance cutters, eight patrol boats, a buoy tender, four Port Security Units, National Strike Force personnel, and two maintenance support units. Nearly half of our selected reserves were brought on active duty to carry out homeland security and national defense missions at home and abroad. At the publishing of this document, six years after the initial conflict, six Coast Guard patrol boats remain in the Persian Gulf conducting coastal sea control and protecting Iraq's oil infrastructure.

The *USCGC Boutwell* patrols near the Kwar al Amaya oil terminal as part of Operation Iraqi Freedom.

Several initiatives begun after September 11, 2001, have helped the Coast Guard in multiple mission areas. The Coast Guard is now an official member of the 16-agency U.S. Intelligence Community. This greatly expands national intelligence resources by adding important elements such as Maritime Intelligence Fusion Centers and field intelligence collectors located with Coast Guard Sectors across the country. No longer will activity at sea be completely anonymous and unmonitored.

The National Maritime Intelligence Center in Maryland.

The Coast Guard also has created Maritime Safety and Security Teams. These are specialized federal maritime enforcement teams assigned to strategically located ports across the United States. They are rapidly deployable by air, sea, or ground to meet emerging contingencies including natural disasters. In addition, the Coast Guard established a highly trained and rapidly deployable Maritime Security Response Team. This team can respond to a broad range of high-threat scenarios, from opposed vessel boardings to actual or potential weapon of mass destruction attacks. These teams and other deployable specialized forces now operate under a single command, the Deployable Operations Group (DOG).

Disaster Strikes the Gulf: Hurricanes Katrina and Rita

Hurricane Katrina struck the Gulf States on August 29, 2005, devastating a 90,000 square mile area from Grand Isle, Louisiana, to

Mobile, Alabama. It was one of the worst natural disasters in American history, with over 1,200 deaths and $80 billion in property damage. The enormous storm surge and subsequent, multiple levee breaches flooded over 60 percent of New Orleans. Tens of thousands of men, women, and children were left stranded on rooftops and in city buildings with no food, water, or electricity.

A Coast Guard helicopter crew lifts stranded victims from their rooftop in the aftermath of Hurricane Katrina.

The massive response that followed was the largest search and rescue operation in U.S. history. Over 5,000 Coast Guard men and women from around the country rescued more than 33,000 people. They also responded to thousands of oil spills totaling over nine million gallons, repaired navigational aids, and restored waterways in and around some of the country's most vital ports.

The Coast Guard has proven agility and significant experience in leading integrated joint-agency operations. Due largely to this, the Coast Guard's Chief of Staff was chosen as Principal Federal Official in the early days of the disaster to coordinate the massive federal, state, and local response to Hurricane Katrina, and subsequently Hurricane Rita.

Hurricanes Katrina and Rita tested the Coast Guard's organizational character. These events once again illustrated our Service's unique national value: Complementary missions and skills, core values and competencies, and deeply ingrained principles of operation enabled the Coast Guard to rise to the moment.

Cooperative Maritime Security for the 21st Century

We live in an interconnected and interdependent world. In this context, the sea services of the United States must work together more closely than ever to ensure the safety and security of the maritime system.

In October 2007, the Navy, Marine Corps, and Coast Guard marked an historical first, signing a unified maritime strategy called "A Cooperative Strategy for 21st Century Seapower." This strategy commits U.S. maritime forces to the full spectrum of operations that

A Cooperative Strategy for 21st Century Seapower

A small boat from *USCGC Dallas* flies a Cape Verdian flag while en route to conduct a multi-national fisheries law enforcement boarding off the coast of São Vicente, Republic of Cape Verde.

advance peace and order, and thus the prosperity and security of our Nation.

Today, the Coast Guard is assisting sailors and marines in the U.S. Navy-led African Partnership Station, to improve the maritime governance of African nations and foster cooperation among their countries and with the United States. While deployed with the U.S. Navy Sixth Fleet in 2008, the *USCGC Dallas* conducted theater security cooperation with maritime law enforcement officers from Cape Verde, Sao Tome and Principe, Gabon, Equatorial Guinea, Ghana, and Senegal. These efforts included the first ever joint law enforcement activities in western Africa when the *Dallas* embarked a law enforcement team from Cape Verde to enforce fisheries regulations within their EEZ. The Coast Guard was also closely involved in international efforts to combat piracy off the Horn of Africa in 2008 and 2009, working with the Navy in both international engagement and tactical law enforcement.

Our national security and prosperity require a close bond among the sea services, now and into the future. Over two centuries of growth, evolution, and experience have prepared the Coast Guard to provide its unique contribution to this team.

Echoes From The Past

By virtue of its history and experience, the Coast Guard has evolved into a multi-mission service that is focused on the full spectrum of maritime affairs. Reflections of this generalist outlook can be seen in the organization, training, and force structure of the modern Coast Guard. Unlike other services, the Coast Guard has no specialized staff corps. Likewise, as a relatively small service with a limited budget, the Coast Guard has needed durable platforms that are flexible enough for many different types of missions.

As the country's maritime "jack of all trades," the Coast Guard has always needed to maintain a high degree of flexibility and operational readiness. Now, in the early years of a new century, the Coast Guard's broad and evolving charter is particularly appropriate for the range of maritime challenges ahead. An integral and essential component of the Department of Homeland Security—but retaining its distinctive identity as a separate "military service and a branch of the Armed Forces of the United States at all times"[48]—the Coast Guard remains *Semper Paratus*—"Always Ready"—to do the Nation's bidding.

USCGC Bertholf approaches *USCGC Eagle* in the San Francisco Bay. *Bertholf* is the Coast Guard's first National Security Cutter—the flagship of the Coast Guard fleet. *Eagle*, a three-masted sailing barque used to train Coast Guard Academy cadets, is the only active commissioned sailing vessel in the U.S. Armed Forces.

The Guardian Ethos

I am America's Maritime Guardian.
I serve the citizens of the United States.
I will protect them.
I will defend them.
I will save them.
I am their Shield.
For them I am *Semper Paratus*.
I live the Coast Guard Core Values.
I am a Guardian.
We are the United States Coast Guard.

Chapter Three

The Nature Of Our Service

*T*he nature of our Service has evolved with the accumulation of new roles and missions from a variety of sources, including executive orders, congressional action, and the absorption of several agencies. These additional roles and missions were assigned for a very pragmatic reason: we were able to perform them effectively and efficiently.

In assuming this succession of new duties, we also developed a unique and distinct character, one shaped by our ethos, core values, and our military, multi-mission, and maritime nature.[49]

Ethos

An ethos is the natural spirit of a community or people. It is the characteristic tone or genius of an institution or social organization.

At the heart of the Coast Guard ethos is the belief that every man and woman in our Service is a guardian. To guard is to watch over or protect from harm.

The origin of our ethos lies in the rich heritage and noble tradition of those who have guarded coasts for millennia. In fact the earliest recorded reference to a coast guard may be on a clay tablet found in the remains of the Palace of Nestor—in Greece—and dating to 1600 to 1200 B.C. This tablet reports "thus the watchers are guarding the coast."[50]

The Guardian Ethos is the contract the Coast Guard and its members make with the nation and its people to be "Always Ready" to protect them—now and in the future.

Core Values

Core values are the accepted principles or standards of a person or a group.

Our core values of Honor, Respect, and Devotion to Duty[51] are deeply rooted in the legacy of service that distinguishes the U.S. Coast Guard. From revenue cutter crews protecting a fledgling Nation from privateers and smugglers, to sturdy surfmen fighting howling gales to rescue shipwrecked mariners, to heroic lighthouse keepers who saved countless lives by dutifully tending their lights and fog signals, to gallant boat coxswains landing Marines at Guadalcanal, to the men and women of today who protect our Nation's waterways and ports, stop smugglers, rescue desperate migrants, and protect endangered marine species, Coast Guard people have embraced and lived these values.

Coast Guard Core Values

Honor – Integrity is our standard. We demonstrate uncompromising ethical conduct and moral behavior in all of our personal and organizational actions. We are loyal and accountable to the public trust.

Respect – We value our diverse workforce. We treat each other and those we serve with fairness, dignity, respect, and compassion. We encourage individual opportunity and growth. We encourage creativity through empowerment. We work as a team.

Devotion to Duty – We are professionals, military and civilian, who seek responsibility, and accept accountability, and are committed to the successful achievement of our organizational goals. We exist to serve. We serve with pride.

The Coast Guard Honor Guard stands in formation before the beginning of the Coast Guard's Veteran's Day wreath-laying ceremony at Arlington National Cemetery.

U.S. Coast Guard Station Golden Gate conducts surf drills in 14-foot seas. The station routinely conducts surf drills to allow their surfmen to re-qualify. Surfmen are the Coast Guard's most experienced and qualified small boat operators.

Our core values are the bedrock upon which our character and operating principles are built. They provide fundamental guidance for our actions, both on duty and in our private lives. They challenge us to live up to the high standards of excellence exhibited by our predecessors. Whether active duty, reserve, civilian, or auxiliary, our core values bind us together and guide our conduct, performance, and decisions.

A Military, Multi-Mission, Maritime Service

We call ourselves a "military," "multi-mission," and "maritime" service. These three descriptors provide a basis for understanding the character and structure of the Coast Guard. We trace their origin to Alexander Hamilton.

Hamilton first proposed a maritime service in 1787. In Federalist Paper No. 12, he suggested a law enforcement organization of "a few armed vessels, judiciously stationed at the entrances of our ports, might at a small expense be made useful sentinels of the laws."

In early 1790, the House of Representatives requested Secretary of the Treasury Hamilton recommend improvements to existing laws imposing duties on imported goods. Hamilton's handwritten report dated April 22, 1790, is remarkable for its vision and persuasive argument to establish a seagoing service that would become the Coast Guard (see Appendix B).

Hamilton reasoned the service should be military in nature, as this "...will not only induce fit men, the more readily to engage, but will attach them to their duties by a nicer sense of honor." He foresaw the multi-mission potential of the organization, "...the utility of which will increase in proportion as the public exigencies may require an augmentation of [its] duties."

These characteristics—military, multi-mission, and maritime—have endured and grown stronger over our complex and varied history. They are also critical to understanding the Coast Guard's role as a unique instrument of America's national security.

Military

Hamilton's report of April 1790 persuaded Congress to act. On August 4, 1790, the Tariff Act established the Revenue Marine and authorized revenue cutters. Hamilton organized the new service along military lines, and convinced President George Washington to commission Revenue Marine officers.

The 1915 legislation establishing the Coast Guard recognized again that military discipline and training were critical for the Coast Guard's national defense duties. Title 14 of the U.S. Code specifies the Coast Guard is a military service and a branch of the Armed Forces of the United States at all times, not just in wartime or when the President directs.

The military profession is like no other. Members of the military voluntarily relinquish some of their freedoms—including even their constitutional right to freedom of speech—in order to serve. Likewise, service members cannot just quit; they must continue to serve until their term is complete and must obey all lawful orders while doing so. Those orders may include undertaking tasks likely to result in members giving the last full measure of devotion—their lives—in service to our country. This requirement sets military

The *USCGC Maui* and *USCGC Monomoy* as they were being loaded onto a larger ship for transport to the Persian Gulf. The patrol boats and their crews conduct maritime security and interdiction, search and rescue, and local training in support of Operation Iraqi Freedom.

people apart from the members of every other profession. Military forces are also charged with carrying out the systematic application of violence in service to the Nation. As members of an armed force, we are called to act in accordance with these responsibilities, and we have always done so.

The Coast Guard has participated in all our nation's wars as a naval augmentation force, providing specialized capabilities as required for the defense of our nation. However, the national security environment has changed since the end of the Cold War and since terrorists struck our country. Coast Guard military missions today are sometimes extensions of our peacetime duties. Peacetime military engagement, maritime security operations, and humanitarian assistance—areas of traditional Coast Guard expertise—have risen in significance within the spectrum of military operations.

These specialized capabilities that allow us to augment the U.S. Navy also distinguish us from that service. The purpose of the Navy is set forth in Title 10 of the U.S. Code: "The Navy shall be organized, trained, and equipped primarily for prompt and sustained combat incident to operations at sea." [52]

Signalman First Class
Douglas A. Munro
Medal of Honor Citation

"For extraordinary heroism and conspicuous gallantry in action above and beyond the call of duty as Officer-in-Charge of a group of Higgins boats, engaged in the evacuation of a Battalion of Marines trapped by enemy Japanese forces at Point Cruz, Guadalcanal, on September 27, 1942. After making preliminary plans for the evacuation of nearly 500 beleaguered Marines, Munro, under constant risk of his life, daringly led five of his small craft toward the shore. As he closed the beach, he signaled [sic] the others to land, and then in order to draw the enemy's fire and protect the heavily loaded boats, he valiantly placed his craft with its two small guns as a shield between the beachhead and the Japanese. When the perilous task of evacuation was nearly completed, Munro was killed by enemy fire, but his crew, two of whom were wounded, carried on until the last boat had loaded and cleared the beach. By outstanding leadership, expert planning, and dauntless devotion to duty, he and his courageous comrades undoubtedly saved the lives of many who otherwise would have perished. He gallantly gave up his life in defense of his country."

Signalman First Class Douglas A. Munro (manning the machine gun in the foreground).

Captain Quentin R. Walsh

Lieutenant Commander (later Captain) Quentin R. Walsh was a member of the logistics and planning section, U.S. Naval Forces in Europe during World War II. He planned the occupation of the port of Cherbourg, France, which was viewed as vital to the invading allied forces and their resupply effort.

Lieutenant Commander Walsh's plan called for the formation of a specially trained naval reconnaissance unit to determine the condition of the port after its capture. While leading the 53-man special mission to the port of Cherbourg, he and his men met up with the U.S. 79th Infantry Division and joined them in fierce house-to-house fighting against the Germans. The Allied forces quickly captured the eastern part of the port, while most of the Germans retreated to the western section of the city.

Lieutenant Commander Walsh personally led a 16-member unit of his special task force on a raid to an arsenal area and adjacent waterfront on the western side of the city. Armed with bazookas, hand grenades, rifles, and submachine guns, he and his party overcame sniper fire to capture underground bunkers and approximately 400 Germans in the arsenal area. Lieutenant Commander Walsh's command went on to capture Fort Du Homet and its garrison of 350 men. Upon entering the fort, he convinced the Germans that the city had already fallen. He then accepted the surrender of 300 German troops and liberated 50 American paratroopers who had been prisoners since D-Day. Lieutenant Commander Walsh received the Navy Cross for his heroic actions.

Captain
Quentin R.
Walsh

The Navy is not equipped, structured, or authorized to execute the domestic maritime governance and security operations we routinely handle. Unlike the Coast Guard, the Navy is constrained by the *Posse Comitatus* doctrine, which prevents the other military services from acting as law enforcement agents on U.S. soil, in U.S. territorial waters, or against U.S. citizens.[53] By the same token, the Coast Guard is not organized, trained, and equipped to engage in the full spectrum of naval operations. Hence, far from being duplicative, the Coast Guard, Navy, and Marine Corps instead provide resources that mutually support and complement each other's roles and missions in order to satisfy the entire spectrum of America's maritime needs.

Because the Coast Guard is a military service, our cutters are designated as warships of the United States. This status affords our ships certain rights under international conventions and practice, such as the right to approach any vessel to ascertain its identity and country of origin. It gives our vessels sovereign immunity vis-à-vis other countries' laws.

Multi-Mission

We fulfill our three broad roles—**maritime safety, security, and stewardship**—by accomplishing a set of 11 supporting missions. All Coast Guard missions—whether ensuring the security of America's harbors and ports, rescuing distressed mariners, interdicting drug smugglers, combating major oil spills, or conducting naval warfare missions in support of the unified combatant commanders—contribute directly to the economic, environmental, and physical security of the United States.

As noted earlier, most missions support more than one role. This multi-functional capability is an enduring Coast Guard quality. Our ability to field versatile platforms and develop multitalented Coast Guard men and women is perhaps our most important strength. In short, we uphold all of America's maritime interests, including national defense.

We are the Nation's at-sea law enforcement arm, with the broad authority of Section 89 of Title 14 U.S. Code. Our reach extends to undocumented migrant interdiction, drug interdiction, and fisheries protection. Our versatile deepwater cutters stand the watch with a ready flight deck, a boat at the rail, and a trained boarding party always ready to enforce domestic law, observe international standards, and preserve individual human rights. With a long history of carrying out these roles and missions, the Coast Guard stands ready to ensure homeland security at our ports and maritime borders.

The Coast Guard's buoy tender fleet presents a classic example of our multi-mission nature. In addition to setting buoys to ensure the safe navigation of mariners, these cutters deploy oil containment booms to protect the environment, break ice for domestic maritime traffic, conduct naval warfare duties, interdict drugs and undocumented migrants, and perform search and rescue and law enforcement missions.

The *USCGC Anthony Petit* deploys oil spill containment boom during a training exercise in Ketchikan, Alaska.

Our Coast Guard Sectors are also multi-mission capable. Sector personnel respond to mariners in distress, enforce federal laws, and support other federal, state, local, and tribal authorities. They also inspect vessels and facilities for compliance with safety, security, and environmental laws. They restrict access to vessels and facilities when necessary for national security or public safety purposes. They enforce pollution prevention statutes and respond to hazardous substance releases and discharges of oil and refuse into our navigable waters. And Sector personnel supervise or control vessel movement in America's ports and waterways, and investigate marine casualties.

Maritime

The maritime region is the Coast Guard's domain. Everything we do—whether domestically or internationally—has a maritime connection.

Given America's historic and continuing dependence on the sea, the creation of a force focused on maritime—though not strictly military—tasks was inevitable. Maritime trade has always played a key role in the Nation's economic health. Whether transporting dry bulk cargo, petroleum products, passengers, or containerized cargo, ships will continue to provide a cost-effective method of transportation. Their safe and efficient movement will be an important necessity for the United States. Likewise, fish and fishing fleets have been crucial to the American diet and economy. And as the Nation has grown wealthier, cruise ships, floating casinos, and recreational boats have joined traditional commercial users of U.S. domestic waterways in ever-greater numbers.

A Humanitarian Reputation

The Coast Guard is renowned throughout the world for saving lives. The same military discipline that serves the Coast Guard well in war, serves it equally well in peace. Nowhere is this more apparent than in the prosecution of search and rescue cases. Our reputation is based on personal courage and selflessness that goes back to the earliest days of the disparate Life-Saving, Lighthouse, and Revenue Cutter Services. Our history is replete with heroes such as Joshua James, Ida Lewis, Captain Josiah Sturgis, the Pea Island Station crew, and countless others who risked their lives repeatedly to save mariners in distress. Nothing fills us with greater pride than the stories of harrowing rescues in which professional Coast Guard men and women returned would-be victims safely to their families, against all odds. It is no accident that these are stories of success. Preparation for the moment—born of excellent training, support, and equipment blended with courage, discipline, and selflessness—is our hallmark.

Our humanitarian reputation, however, goes beyond the search and rescue mission. Whether responding to an oil spill, providing relief supplies to victims of war or natural disasters, ensuring safe marine transportation, conducting peacetime engagement visits to foreign countries, or working with international organizations to improve the safety of commercial shipping, our Service reflects a commitment to serving others on a daily basis. These activities add a distinctive humanitarian dimension to our character, and help define who we are.

A Coast Guard HC-130 airplane and crew delivers over 34,000 pounds of food to the tsunami affected town of Jaffna, Sri Lanka in January 2005. Coast Guard units from Air Stations Clearwater, Florida; Elizabeth City, North Carolina; Barbers Point, Hawaii; and Sacramento, California, deployed to Southeast Asia to deliver aid.

Captain Richard Etheridge and the Pea Island Life-Saving Crew

On January 24, 1880, Captain Richard Etheridge became the first African-American to command a U.S. Life-Saving Station when the Service appointed him as the Keeper of the Pea Island Life-Saving Station, near Cape Fear, North Carolina. Soon after Etheridge's appointment, he supervised the construction of a new station and developed rigorous lifesaving drills that enabled his crew to hone their skills. The Pea Island Station quickly earned the reputation as "one of the tautest on the Carolina Coast," with Etheridge known as one of the most courageous and ingenious lifesavers in the Service.

On October 11, 1896, Etheridge's rigorous training drills proved to be invaluable. The three-masted schooner, *E.S. Newman*, was caught in a hurricane while en route from Providence, Rhode Island, to Norfolk, Virginia. The ship lost all sails and was blown 100 miles south off course before it ran aground near Pea Island.

Etheridge and his crew quickly swung into action, hitching mules to the beach cart and hurrying toward the vessel. Arriving on scene, they found the vessel's captain and eight others clinging to the wreckage. High water prevented them from firing a line to the schooner with a Lyle gun, so Etheridge directed two surfmen to bind themselves together with a line. Grasping a second line, the pair fought through the

The Pea Island Life-Saving Station crew: (left to right) Richard Etheridge, Benjamin Bowser, Dorman Pugh, Theodore Meekins, Lewis Wescott, Stanley Wise, and William Irving.

breakers while the remaining surfmen secured the other end on shore. The two surfmen reached the wreck and, using a heaving stick, got the line on board. Once a line was tied around one of the crewmen, all three were then pulled back through the surf by the crew on the beach. After each trip, two different surfmen replaced those who had just returned. The seemingly inexhaustible Pea Island lifesavers journeyed through the perilous waters a total of ten times, rescuing the entire crew of the *E.S. Newman*.

For their efforts, the all-African-American crew of the Pea Island Life-Saving Station—Richard Etheridge, Benjamin Bowser, Dorman Pugh, Theodore Meekins, Lewis Wescott, Stanley Wise, and William Irving—were awarded the Gold Lifesaving Medal posthumously on March 5, 1996. Richard Etheridge died while in service on May 8, 1900.

A Unique Service

Taken together, the Coast Guard's status as an armed force, its law enforcement authorities, and its reputation for humanitarian service, gives us a breadth of access unique among the agencies of the United States. Because of this unique character, U.S. presidents have often found the Coast Guard to be a readily available and useful instrument for responding to national emergencies or enforcing national policy. In addition, we "speak the language" of both civil and military organizations. We can play an important bridging role by coordinating the actions of U.S. and foreign civilian agencies and military forces in the maritime arena. The Coast Guard can provide the needed presence, access, and influence in nations where humanitarian and constabulary skills are most needed.

Our status as a military force with many civilian duties and responsibilities was closely reviewed at the time the Life-Saving Service and Revenue Cutter Service were merged to become the U.S. Coast Guard in 1915. Captain-Commandant Ellsworth Price Bertholf— the last Commandant of the Revenue Cutter Service and the first Commandant of the newly formed U.S. Coast Guard—forthrightly discussed the nature of the newly created Service in his first annual report to Congress:

> *The Coast Guard occupies a peculiar position among other branches of the Government, and necessarily so from the dual character of its work, which is both civil and military. Its organization, therefore, must be such as will best adapt it to the performance of both classes of duties, and as a civil organization would not suffice for the performance of military functions, the organization of the service must be and is by law military. More than 120 years of practical experience has demonstrated that it is by means of military drills, training, and discipline that the service is enabled to maintain that state of preparedness for the prompt performance of its most important civil duties, which...are largely of an emergent nature.*[54]

Captain-Commandant Bertholf's statement is no less true today. Coast Guard men and women perform well because they prepare well. In the final analysis, the Coast Guard's legal core is as a military service, invested with unique law enforcement authorities and leavened with a well-earned reputation for humanitarian service. These singular attributes enable us to satisfy a broad, multi-mission mandate from our nation. Our core values of Honor, Respect, and Devotion to Duty are key to fulfilling that mandate. As **America's Maritime Guardian,** we are proud to be warriors and protectors—guardians at all times.

Lieutenant Colleen A. Cain

Lieutenant Colleen A. Cain became the Service's third female aviator and the first female helicopter pilot in June 1979. In her brief career, Cain flew many rescue missions and completed her qualifications as Co-pilot, First Pilot, and Aircraft Commander. In 1980, she received the Coast Guard Achievement Medal for saving a three-year-old boy involved in a boating accident.

Lieutenant
Colleen A. Cain

In the early morning hours of January 7, 1982, while stationed at Air Station Barbers Point, Hawaii, Cain took flight in severe weather, heavy winds, and limited visibility in response to a distress call from a sinking fishing vessel with seven persons on board. While en route to the sinking vessel, the HH-52A helicopter she was co-piloting crashed into the side of a mountain in the Wailua Valley of Molokai, Hawaii, killing Cain and her two crewmembers, Lieutenant Commander Buzz Johnson and Aviation Survivalman David Thompson. Cain became the first female Coast Guard member killed in the line of duty. A Coast Guard officer wrote of Cain's reputation among her peers: "Without fail, they regarded her as an exemplary Coast Guard officer, patriot, and human being."

Lieutenant Cain and her fellow crewmembers made the ultimate sacrifice in service to their nation and fellow countrymen, striving to protect life at sea. On October 25, 1985, the Coast Guard dedicated Cain Hall, a 100-room residence hall at Training Center Yorktown, Virginia, to her memory.

Damage Controlman Third Class
Nathan B. Bruckenthal
Bronze Star Medal Citation

"For heroic achievement in connection with combat operations against the enemy while serving as Boarding Officer with USS Firebolt (PC 10) and United State Coast Guard Law Enforcement Detachment 403 during Operating Iraqi Freedom on 24 April 2004. While patrolling the security zone around the Al Basra Oil terminal in Iraqi territorial waters, Petty Officer Bruckenthal detected a small, unidentified dhow proceeding towards the Oil Terminal. After maneuvering the team to screen the oil terminal, Petty Officer Bruckenthal approached the dhow to investigate its actions. As the boarding team drew alongside the dhow, the attacker on board the vessel, realizing he had been discovered, detonated explosives packed on board, mortally wounding Petty Officer Bruckenthal. The explosion alerted all in the area to an ongoing coordinated attack, allowing security forces to destroy two additional explosives laden vessels, thereby preventing massive casualties, irreversible environmental damage, and the destruction of the Iraqi peoples' major economic lifeline. By his zealous initiative, courageous actions, and exceptional dedication to duty, Petty Officer Bruckenthal reflected great credit upon himself and upheld the highest traditions of the Coast Guard and the United States Naval Service."

Damage Controlman Third Class Nathan B. Bruckenthal

Chapter Four

Principles of Coast Guard Operations

*O*ur effectiveness as a military, multi-mission, and maritime service depends in no small part on a set of key ideas about the way we operate. These principles trace their roots to our birth as the Revenue Marine (See Appendix C). They have strengthened over time and now reflect the essence of our Service culture. They describe our operating style and underpin our ability to perform successfully, both domestically and internationally.

Principles of Coast Guard Operations

- **Clear Objective**
- **Effective Presence**
- **Unity of Effort**
- **On-Scene Initiative**
- **Flexibility**
- **Managed Risk**
- **Restraint**

The Coast Guard's operating principles encompass both the civil and military elements of our roles and missions. As a military service at all times, the Coast Guard subscribes to the Principles of Joint Operations codified in joint service doctrine. The principles of Coast Guard operations complement the principles of joint operations and accommodate the distinctions between war-fighting and civil law enforcement and regulation.

The principles of Coast Guard operations discussed below apply across the range of Service roles and missions. There will be times, during engagements with clearly hostile forces for instance, when the importance of some of these principles will decrease. Nevertheless, these principles guide our actions in the vast majority of situations we encounter.

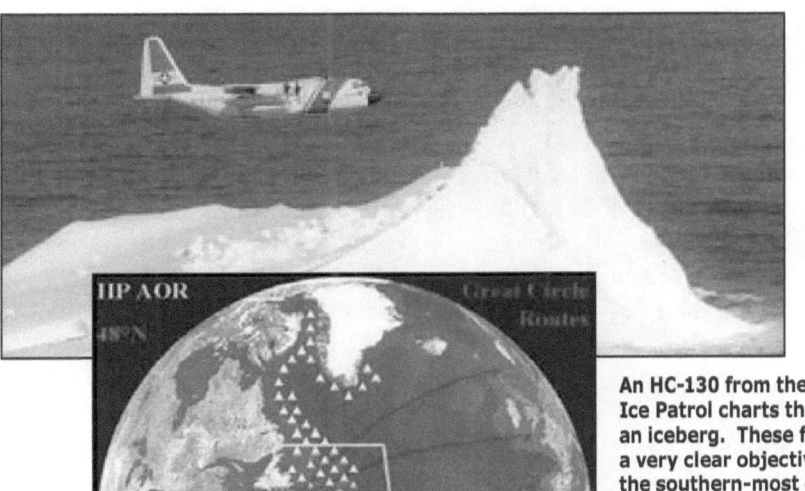

An HC-130 from the International Ice Patrol charts the location of an iceberg. These flights have a very clear objective: To track the southern-most extent of all known ice in the North Atlantic. This information allows ships to steer clear of dangerous icebergs.

The Principle of Clear Objective

Every operation should be directed toward a clearly defined and attainable objective. The most significant action a leader can take in planning and executing an operation is to express the overarching objective clearly to subordinates. This principle holds whether the objective is one that has been defined by our national leaders, or by the commander on-scene at an oil spill or some other operation. Once the objective has been defined, we must focus our operations, plans, and efforts on achieving it.

Some operations are short-lived, and the objectives are easily understood. Rescue the people. Prevent the spill. Clean up the spill. Seize the drugs. Other operations are of a long-term nature, and the objectives may not be as easily defined. For example, the primary focus of a cutter on patrol may be fisheries law enforcement. Yet, like a police officer on a beat, a cutter on patrol is also alert and well prepared to perform all other Coast Guard missions. Nonetheless, on-scene commanders must be able to articulate the central objective of the mission at hand.

The Principle of Effective Presence

At the most basic level, effective presence means having the right assets and capabilities at the right place at the right time. This principle traces its origins to the earliest days of the Revenue Marine. The first revenue cutters were designed specifically to be effective in their designated operating areas—rivers, harbors, and their approaches—and they were assigned to the most strategically important ports. The first Revenue Marine officers came from the ranks of the colonial merchant fleet, former privateers, and the former state and Continental navies. They were selected because they understood their operating areas and the methods of their adversaries. This put the "right assets" in place.

Revenue Marine founder Alexander Hamilton explained another aspect of the concept of effective presence in a Letter of Instruction to his officers in 1791:

> [I]t will be necessary for you from time to time to ply along the coasts in the neighborhood of your station, and to traverse the different parts of the waters which it comprehends. To fix yourself constantly or even generally at one position, would in a great measure defeat the purpose of the establishment. It would confine your vigilance to a particular spot, and allow full scope to fraudulent practices, everywhere else.[56]

Hamilton was saying that to be effective, units must be active because the "right place to be" changes over time. This is reflected in the assignment of units to different operating areas depending on the anticipated need. Once assigned, cutters and aircraft need to patrol operating areas, boats need to cruise local waterways, and marine safety personnel need to patrol the port. To be effective, we must be vigilant and ready to respond to situations as they arise, keeping in mind all of our principles of operations.

Ensuring an effective presence also requires careful attention to the ability to sustain our assets during normal operations. We should operate our assets to the level—and only to the level—that the logistics system (i.e., people, parts and equipment, and funding) can sustain. If we can only achieve near-term results by operating

By arming Coast Guard helicopters, we have become much more effective at stopping drug smugglers in "go-fast" boats through the use of warning shots and disabling fire.

our assets beyond the level of long-term sustainability, we risk harming the national interests by degrading our ability to respond effectively in the future.

A key factor in effective presence is its acceptability. Foreign governments and non-governmental organizations often regard Coast Guard forces as welcomed and valued partners. Due to the combination of our military status, our law enforcement authorities, and our reputation for humanitarianism, the Coast Guard offers the United States unique forces with which to pursue national strategies and enforce national policy. Indeed, in many civil and military arenas worldwide, the Coast Guard is ideally suited to cooperate with and provide assistance to foreign governments, navies, coast guards, international organizations, and non-governmental organizations on a broad spectrum of issues.

The Principle of Unity of Effort

Most Coast Guard operations are performed as a cooperative effort among multiple Coast Guard units working in coordination with diverse governmental and non-governmental entities. Achieving successful outcomes requires positive leadership to ensure clear understanding of the objective and the role that each individual, unit, or organization is expected to play in meeting that objective.

Transparency is a concept implicit in unified operations. Units must work with and around one another in an entirely open manner. Actions must be easily interpreted and understood. Lack of transparency can lead to doubt, confusion, or even mistrust. Any of these can cause a mission to fail.

The concept known as the "chain of command" is an essential element in achieving internal unity of effort. The chain of command embodies the principle that every person—and every unit—in a military organization reports to someone higher. In each operation, there can be only one responsible commander. The timely and accurate flow of information to and from that responsible commander via the chain of command is essential for ensuring that needed resources, including information, get to the right place at the right time.

Maintaining an effective and efficient chain of command requires constant attention, because we deploy multi-mission field units under higher-echelon commanders whose staffs are organized along mission or other specialty lines. This calls for a high degree of staff

Members from the FBI Dive Team, NASA, and the Coast Guard National Strike Force search for debris from the Space Shuttle *Columbia* along the shores of the Toledo Bend Reservoir in Texas.

coordination. Respect for the chain of command, especially when coupled with proper staffing, contributes significantly to internal unity of effort.

Hurricanes Katrina and Rita provide a compelling illustration. Coast Guard active duty, reserve, civilian, and auxiliary personnel came together from Coast Guard units around the country and overseas—Alaska, New England, Guam, Puerto Rico, Hawaii, and elsewhere—in an enormous unified response. This unprecedented effort included over 5,000 Coast Guard members, 62 aircraft, 42 cutters, and 131 boats. This unity of effort was key to the rescue of tens of thousands of people after one of the worst natural disasters in U.S. history.

Unity among organizations is the external counterpart to internal unity of effort. The challenge of external leadership is, in many respects, more demanding. The external entities with whom we deal generally are not under the Coast Guard's authority, and discerning lines of authority for those organizations may be difficult. Moreover, the Coast Guard frequently has to decide among the conflicting and divergent demands of various stakeholders, each of whom represents legitimate and worthy public or private interests.

Again, Hurricanes Katrina and Rita are instructive. Through strong relationships with the maritime industry, U.S. Army Corps of Engineers, National Oceanic and Atmospheric Administration, and the U.S. Navy, Coast Guard incident commanders led the rapid assessment and reopening of 255 miles of the Mississippi River and more than 200 miles of the Gulf Intracoastal Waterway. Within four days, deep draft commercial vessels were entering port. The Coast Guard, working with the Environmental Protection Agency, coordinated the work of more than 750 pollution responders, the deployment of more than 30,000 feet of boom, and the recovery of over 3 million gallons of oil.

The Coast Guard does not always have the lead or final authority to make decisions in all situations; we are also comfortable in a support role. Nevertheless, the responsibilities and authorities given to the Coast Guard by Congress, and the tendency of Congresses and Presidents to turn to the Coast Guard whenever difficult maritime issues arise, are testimonies to our history of providing effective leadership across diverse and competing interests.

The Principle of On-Scene Initiative

The nature of our operations demands that Coast Guard men and women be given latitude to act quickly and decisively within the scope of their authority, without waiting for direction from higher levels in the chain of command. Personal initiative has always been crucial to the success of our Service. Tight control from above was never an option for the Revenue Marine, whose original ten cutters were based from Portsmouth, New Hampshire, to Savannah, Georgia; or for the nineteenth century Life-Saving Service, which relied on 148 remote stations along the U.S. coast.[57]

In August 1899, Surfman Rasmus S. Midgett arrived at the scene of the 643-ton barkentine *Priscilla*, which had been broken in two and grounded three miles south of Gull Shoal U.S. Life-Saving Service Station. Ten surviving crewmembers clung to the wreckage. Midgett made a critical decision to make the rescue alone rather than make the three-mile trip back to the station for assistance. Seven of the crewmembers were able to assist in their rescue, but the remaining three were too weak and Rasmus rescued them by struggling to the ship in the heavy surf, placing a crewman on his shoulder and carrying him through the pounding surf. He repeated this action two more times until all were safe. He was later awarded the Gold Lifesaving Medal, the highest award bestowed by the Secretary of the Treasury.

Since then, advances in technology have revolutionized our commanders' ability to communicate with and even control units in the field. But the concept of allowing the person on-scene to take the initiative—guided by a firm understanding of the desired tactical objectives and the national interests at stake—remains central to the Coast Guard's view of its command relationships.

Many of our operations—responding to oil spills, searching for and rescuing mariners in distress, or interdicting smugglers, for instance—are of an emergent, unpredictable nature. History has shown that situations like these are best handled locally. Thus, we push both authority and responsibility to the lowest possible level. Our belief is that the person on scene can be depended upon to assess the situation, seize the initiative, and take the actions necessary for success.

This style of operational command is based upon the trust that senior commanders place in their subordinates' judgment. Decisive action requires unity of effort—getting all parts of a force to work together. Rapid action, on the other hand, requires a large degree of decentralization, giving those closest to the problem the freedom to solve it. To reconcile these seemingly contradictory requirements, we use the tools known as the "commander's intent" and the "concept of operations."

The commander's intent conveys the objective and the desired course of action. The concept of operations details the commander's estimated sequence of actions to achieve the objective and contains essential elements of a plan, i.e., what is to be done, and how the commander plans to do it. A significant change in the situation that requires new action will alter the concept of operations, but the commander's intent—their overriding objective—usually remains unchanged.

Effective commanders at all levels neither expect, nor attempt to control, their subordinates' every action. Instead, they make sure that subordinates thoroughly understand their expectations and how to meet those expectations in a variety of situations. Great commanders in naval history rarely issued detailed instructions to their subordinate commanders. Instead, they frequently gathered their captains to discuss a variety of tactical problems. Through these informal discussions, the captains became aware of what their commanders expected to accomplish and how they planned to accomplish it in a range of situations. Thus, the subordinates were prepared to act independently, in accordance with their commander's intent, even though formal orders were brief or nonexistent.

Good decisions are made in unpredictable situations when Coast Guard personnel on the scene of an emergency or a crisis are trained rigorously to act as part of a cohesive, cooperative team. It is achieved through the common understanding of how individual incidents or situations are normally handled. This shared understanding lies at the heart of effective, decentralized command and control.

The Principle of Flexibility

The revenue cutter *Bear*, veteran of 34 cruises to Alaskan waters during the late 19th and early 20th century. The *Bear* represented the first significant federal government presence in Alaska after the U.S. Government purchased it, and the crew conducted a wide range of activities for the Alaskan people.

This principle is the operational corollary of our multi-mission character. Arising from a combination of broad authority, diverse responsibilities, and limited resources, the flexibility principle implies that if we are to succeed in pursuing multiple missions with common assets and personnel, we must be able to adjust to a wide variety of tasks and circumstances.

As is true of our other principles of operations, the principle of flexibility has its roots in our early history. During their operations in Alaska during the nineteenth century, for example, the crew of the revenue cutter *Bear* conducted an incredible variety of tasks, including the transporting of reindeer and undertaking long, arduous rescue missions through the territory's interior. Many of these tasks went well beyond anything they could have imagined from their original orders. Thanks to their training, experience, and can-do attitude, crew members were able to adapt their operations to answer the needs of the people they served.

This notion of flexibility is also deeply embedded in the Coast Guard's motto, "*Semper Paratus.*" We built our reputation for being "Always Ready" to meet any maritime challenge by successfully and repeatedly adapting to the situation at hand. Thus, a cutter on fisheries patrol is as prepared to divert to a search and rescue operation, respond to a pollution incident, or intercept a suspected drug smuggler—perhaps across thousands of nautical miles of open ocean—as it is to enforce fisheries laws.

Our units frequently face competing mission priorities as incidents unfold. Two examples illustrate the point. A cruise ship on fire and drifting toward the rocks is both a search and rescue case, and a potential pollution incident. Similarly, an overloaded boat filled with migrants intent on reaching our shores is both a law enforcement and a potential search and rescue case. In each instance, responding units must adapt to the circumstances as they unfold, giving priority to the mission most critical at the moment.

> ## The Origins of *Semper Paratus*
>
> The exact origin of our motto—*Semper Paratus*—never has been determined. The earliest recorded use of the phrase *Semper Paratus* in regards to the Service was in the New Orleans newspaper, *Bee*, in January 1836, which used the phrase in an article praising the revenue cutter *Ingham*. The motto appears to have been adopted between October 1896 and May 1897, when a new seal containing the phrase appeared on a general order of the Division of Revenue Cutter Service on May 21, 1897.

The most demanding circumstances we face today require the Coast Guard to conduct "surge operations"—high-intensity efforts usually launched on short notice in response to an emergency situation. Significant examples of events requiring surge operations include the *Exxon Valdez* oil spill response in 1989, the mass migrations from Haiti and Cuba that occurred in 1992 and 1994, and the massive port security effort following the terrorist attacks of September 11, 2001.

Surge operations require the Coast Guard to re-allocate large numbers of people, assets, and money to respond to emerging situations. This affects not only the people and units directly involved, but also demands that the entire Service adapt to find the resources to meet the needs of the surge operation while still continuing critical day-to-day operations. Upon completion of the surge, the Coast Guard then must transition back to normal operations. Surge operations are very demanding, but our ability to flow forces in an emergency provides an enormous benefit to the Nation, and serves as a testament to our flexibility.

The Principle of Managed Risk

Just as the unity of effort principle has both internal and external aspects, so too the principle of managed risk operates at two levels. The internal aspect of this principle involves the commander's obligations to ensure their unit is properly trained, equipped, and maintained for its mission. The commander must also measure crew and equipment capabilities carefully against the operational scenario when assessing whether and how to execute a given mission.

We do dangerous work in hostile environments. Our heritage is based in large part on the selfless acts of courageous men and women who used their capabilities and their wits under hazardous conditions to save the lives of others. This tradition continues today as we perform duties that routinely place us in harm's way. Without a continuing and observable commitment to the safety of our forces, we unnecessarily endanger our people and jeopardize the mission.

Members of Sector Houston-Galveston work in an incident command post to prepare for Hurricane Ike. These preparations will be critical to safeguarding Coast Guard responders and equipment. They will also ensure those in need will receive Coast Guard assistance as soon as possible during or after the storm.

Successful mission execution begins with a thorough understanding of the environment in which we operate. Based on that understanding, we develop operational concepts, acquire appropriate equipment, and put our people through rigorous formal preparation. We build on that foundation by continuous training and drills, by improving our personal operational and support skills, and by maintaining our equipment at the highest state of readiness. The Coast Guard's entire system of operations and support ensures our organizational readiness to carry out our missions; and as our readiness increases, our risks decrease. In short, consistently successful performance requires thorough preparation.

Preparation alone, however, is not enough. Success also requires that our people and equipment be used within the limits of their capabilities. No boat or aircraft, no matter how well maintained or skillfully piloted, can be expected to survive, much less execute a mission, when wind and sea conditions are beyond the strength of hull, airframe, or the human crew. Responsible commanders evaluate the capability of crew and equipment against the conditions likely to be encountered when deciding on the proper course of action. Conscious attention to time-tested and time-honored principles of safe operation is a necessity.

The standard of response in today's Coast Guard remains consistent with our rich legacy. We honor our heritage daily by casting off all lines or lifting off in severe weather. We accept the risk that comes with protecting our nation, saving lives, and rescuing property in peril. We understand the possibility that we may not come back. We honor our heritage as well by attending to the principle that a proper and practiced understanding of duties, a thorough evaluation of the risks involved in an operation, and the exercise of good judgment in executing that operation are of paramount importance for success.

The idea of managing risks is not limited to Coast Guard response operations. In fact, managing risk through prevention (to reduce the probability of an adverse event) and response (to minimize consequences when an adverse event does occur) has long been a fundamental aspect of Coast Guard operations. Prevention includes such measures as placing aids to navigation in shipping channels; ensuring that commercial vessels are properly designed, built, and maintained; and providing courtesy marine exams and safety education for recreational boaters. Prevention will never be perfect. So we maintain the ability to respond aggressively and capably to adverse events, whether in a search and rescue situation or following an oil spill. We also use these same prevention and response concepts internally. We acquire rugged ships, boats, and aircraft, and train our crews with prevention in mind. We also monitor unfolding operations and have backup plans in place, ready to minimize negative consequences when the unanticipated does occur.

Finally, prevention and response activities, while focused on different aspects of the same problem, are inextricably linked. Neither is superior to the other, and neither is adequate by itself. More importantly, the Coast Guard's overall effectiveness depends on the synergy between these two very different means of achieving success: our operational strengths in the response arena make us more effective in the prevention arena, and vice versa. Preparation, prevention, and response are essential tools for Coast Guard success.

The Principle of Restraint

Coast Guard personnel have always been under a special obligation to exercise their powers prudently and with restraint. Section 89 of Title 14 U.S. Code, confers on Coast Guard personnel an unparalleled level of law enforcement authority. Consequently, the portion of Treasury Secretary Hamilton's Letter of Instruction to Revenue Cutter officers, explaining the need for restraint and the standard to be met, remains as true today as in 1791:

> *[A]lways keep in mind that [your] countrymen are free men and, as such, are impatient of everything that bears the least mark of a domineering spirit ... [Refrain, therefore,] with the most guarded circumspection, from whatever has the semblance of haughtiness, rudeness, or insult ... [E]ndeavor to overcome difficulties, if any are experienced, by a cool and temperate perseverance in [your] duty—by address and moderation, rather than vehemence and violence.*[58]

The Coast Guard has a legacy of public service that has shaped our tradition of restraint and good judgment. The Life-Saving Service rescued distressed mariners. The Steamboat Inspection Service protected ships' crews, passengers, and cargo. The Lighthouse Service had similar humanitarian commitments. The Revenue Marine cruised offshore in winter to aid mariners. Today, we do all this and more. Our regulatory and law enforcement missions contribute to the safety and wellbeing of the American public. A lack of restraint in Coast Guard operations, then, would be inconsistent with one of the fundamental and longstanding customs of the Service, as well as potentially violating the constitutional protections afforded American citizens.

As in the case of unity of effort, transparency is an important element within the principle of restraint. Our actions should be as open as possible under the circumstances. Openness instills public confidence in our decisions and conduct.

Restraint extends beyond how Coast Guard personnel treat American citizens—it also covers how we treat foreign citizens with whom we come in contact. Our sensitive handling of undocumented migrants during mass exoduses from Cuba and Haiti show that Coast Guard forces can safeguard U.S. interests at sea, while also upholding the dignity and contributing to the well-being of the migrants. As the leading edge of U.S. maritime law enforcement, the Coast Guard must also exercise appropriate restraint when dealing with illegal acts by foreign vessels and their crews. It is our ability to balance restraint against the need for decisive and aggressive action when the Nation's security is threatened that identifies the Coast Guard as a model for the maritime world. We have a duty to enforce U.S. sovereignty, but in a manner that does honor to the Constitution we took an oath to protect and defend.

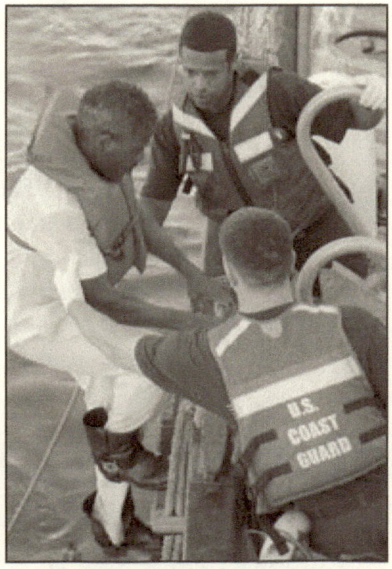

A Dominican Republic undocumented migrant climbs the jacob's ladder to board *USCGC Oak*. While on Coast Guard vessels, migrants receive meals, blankets, and sandals along with medical attention as needed.

Conclusion

Taken together, the characteristics and attributes discussed in this publication define a remarkable institution of high purpose and enduring worth to America. We have developed a culture and sense of ourselves that defines who we are at the start of every day. We are public servants with a duty to benefit society by successfully accomplishing our roles and missions. The Coast Guard is the recipient of public trust, and we must remain worthy of that trust. We recognize that few organizations afford their members as much responsibility and authority at junior levels as does the Coast Guard. Regardless of our rank, rate, or position, we are personally charged with careful stewardship of that authority and the resources that have been delegated to our use.

Whether we are members of a large unit, a small station, or a crew at sea—whether active duty, reservist, civilian, or auxiliarist—we are one Coast Guard. Our Service has many of the positive characteristics of a family-run firm. This permits our personnel and individual units to be nimble and flexible, changing quickly with little effort. Our organization works on the basis of trust among our people; and in turn, their loyalty, sense of responsibility, and professionalism motivate each of us to excel.

As Coast Guard men and women—guardians all—we enthusiastically embrace the heritage of *Semper Paratus* and our responsibility to uphold the values of Honor, Respect, and Devotion to Duty. We are heirs to a proud historical tradition. We understand that by their day-to-day fidelity to these values, our forebears developed and bequeathed to us a venerable institution respected throughout the world for its role as **America's Maritime Guardian.**

A Coast Guard member stands guard near the Brooklyn Bridge.

Appendices

Appendix A: Glossary

These definitions, particularly the ones defining "territorial seas," "high seas," and "exclusive economic zone" are necessarily general in nature, and for most purposes will suffice in understanding the terms and concepts. However, the reader is cautioned that they are not intended to be, nor should they be understood as providing a comprehensive definition that is legally correct in all contexts.

Acceptable Presence – Forward presence by U.S. forces that other countries do not find threatening or objectionable.

Admeasure – To measure the various dimensions, capacities, and tonnage of a ship for official registration.

Aids to Navigation – Equipment used to assist mariners in determining position and warn of dangers and obstructions by providing references such as audio, visual, or electronic signals.

Armed Force(s) – An organized military force of a nation or group of nations.

Automated Mutual-assistance Vessel Rescue (AMVER) System – An international program led by the Coast Guard to provide assistance to any vessel in distress on the high seas. Participating merchant vessels provide sailing plans, periodic position reports, and a list of their vessels' capabilities to the Coast Guard. The AMVER center then supplies a surface picture to rescue centers that contains the position of participating ships in the vicinity of an emergency that can be used to assist a vessel in distress.

Campaign Streamers – 2 ¾-inch wide by 4-foot long cloth ribbons that are attached to the ceremonial standard of our Coast Guard colors. They represent Coast Guard actions—often heroic—in naval engagements throughout the history of our Service. Our earliest campaign streamer is for the Maritime Protection of the New Republic from 1790-1797. The Coast Guard started using campaign streamers in 1968.

Capability – The ability to execute a specified course of action.

Combatant Commander – A commander of one of the unified or specified combatant commands established by the President. There are six regional unified combatant commands covering the globe which include U.S. Africa Command (USAFRICOM), U.S. Central Command (USCENTCOM), U.S. European Command (USEUCOM), U.S. Pacific Command (USPACOM), U.S. Northern Command (USNORTHCOM), and U.S. Southern Command (USSOUTHCOM). There are also four functional unified combatant commands which include U.S. Joint Forces Command (USJFCOM), U.S. Special Operations Command (USSOCOM), U.S. Strategic Command (USSTRATCOM), and U.S. Transportation Command (USTRANSCOM). The chain of command runs from the President to the Secretary of Defense to the combatant commanders.

Command and Control – The exercise of authority and direction by a properly designated commander over assigned and attached forces in the accomplishment of the mission. Command and control functions are performed through an arrangement of personnel, equipment, communications, facilities, and procedures employed by a commander in planning, directing, coordinating, and controlling forces and operations in the accomplishment of the mission.

Culture – The beliefs, customs, and institutions of an organization.

Cutter – The Royal Navy's definition of a cutter was a small warship capable of carrying 8 to 12 cannons. By general usage, the term cutter came to define any vessel of Great Britain's Royal Customs Service and the term was adopted by the U.S. Treasury Department at the creation of the Revenue Marine. Since that time, no matter what the vessel type, the Service has referred to its largest vessels as cutters. Today, among the U.S. Armed Forces, the term cutter uniquely refers to a Coast Guard vessel at least 65 feet in length overall.

Doctrine – Fundamental principles by which military forces or elements thereof guide their actions in support of national objectives. Doctrine is authoritative but requires judgment in application, and provides decision makers and personnel a standard frame of reference. There are four types of Coast Guard doctrine:

Principles and Culture: The overarching guidance communicating the intent, purpose, history, ethos, values, and reason for the existence of the Coast Guard, its missions, and its workforce. For example, principles and culture that drive Coast Guard activities and align them with national objectives are communicated within this document.

Organizational: A series of publications promulgated to communicate unity of effort and guide professional judgment. Organizational doctrine is authoritative but requires judgment in application and influences how forces are organized and trained, as well as how systems and equipment are procured and maintained.

Operational: Guidance on developing and performing mission execution processes and meeting operational standards. It provides operational guidance for subordinate commanders to follow in carrying out routine Coast Guard missions. It is intended to assist subordinate commanders in making resource apportionment decisions.

Support: Guidance on developing and performing mission support activities; delivering required capability; and meeting support standards informed by readiness, operational, and resource priorities. Guides the delivery of full life-cycle support to Coast Guard forces to enable and sustain mission execution.

Domestic – Pertaining to one's own or a particular country.

Exclusive Economic Zone (EEZ) – Waters, seabed, and the subsoil of the seabed seaward of a coastal state's territorial sea and extending no further than 200-nautical miles from the baseline from which the territorial sea is drawn. In this zone, a coastal state may exercise jurisdiction and control over natural resources, both living and nonliving. For a more comprehensive definition of EEZ, see 33 CFR 2.30.

Federal On-Scene Coordinator (FOSC) – The federal official responsible for monitoring or directing responses to specific oil spills and hazardous substance releases reported to the federal government for which the Coast Guard has jurisdiction. The FOSC coordinates all federal efforts with local, state, tribal and regional response communities, and provides support and information to the same communities.

Function – The appropriate or assigned duties, responsibilities, missions, or tasks of an individual, office, or organization.

High Seas – All waters seaward of the territorial sea of the United States and other nations. For a more comprehensive definition of High Seas, see 33 CFR 2.32.

Humanitarian – An adjective describing actions or measures intended to ameliorate human distress or preserve lives and property, without reference to military or security objectives.

Intelligence Community (IC) – A federation of executive branch agencies and organizations that work separately and together to conduct intelligence activities necessary for the conduct of foreign relations and the protection of the national security of the United States. The 16 members named in law are:

Independent	**Department of Defense**
– Central Intelligence Agency	– Air Force Intelligence Surveillance and Reconnaissance Agency
Department of Energy	– Army Military Intelligence
– Office of Intelligence and Counterintelligence	– Defense Intelligence Agency
Department of Homeland Security	– Marine Corps Intelligence Activity
– Office of Intelligence and Analysis	– National Geospatial-Intelligence Agency
– Coast Guard Intelligence and Criminal Investigations Directorate	– National Reconnaissance Office
Department of Justice	– National Security Agency
– Federal Bureau of Investigation	– Office of Naval Intelligence
– Drug Enforcement Administration	**Department of the Treasury**
Department of State	– Office of Terrorism and Financial Intelligence
– Bureau of Intelligence and Research	

Intermodal – An adjective that in the present context describes some manner of transition between different modes of transportation. An "intermodal connection" is a place where cargoes move from one mode of transportation to another, such as a container yard where shipping containers are transferred from ships to trucks or rail cars.

International – Between or among nations or concerned with the relations between nations.

International Maritime Organization (IMO) – A specialized agency of the United Nations consisting of 168 member states. IMO's main task has been to develop and maintain a comprehensive regulatory framework for shipping including safety, security, environmental, legal, and technical cooperation matters.

International Ship and Port Facility Security Code (ISPS) – A 2004 amendment to the Safety of Life at Sea (SOLAS) Convention (1974/1988) on minimum security arrangements that prescribes responsibilities to governments, shipping companies, shipboard personnel, and port and facility personnel to "detect security threats and take preventative measures against security incidents affecting ships or port facilities used in international trade."

Joint – Activities, operations, or organizations in which elements of more than one armed force of the same nation participate.

Marine Transportation System (MTS) – Consists of ocean, coastal, and inland waterways, ports, intermodal connections, vessels, and commercial, military, and recreational users.

Maritime Domain – All areas and things of, on, under, related to, adjacent to, or bordering on a sea, ocean, or other navigable waterway, including all maritime-related activities, infrastructure, people, cargo, and vessels and other conveyances.

Maritime Domain Awareness (MDA) – The effective understanding of anything associated with the global maritime domain that could impact the security, safety, economy, or environment of the United States.

Memorandum of Agreement – An agreement between two or more agencies that governs the terms by which mutually supporting services and responsibilities will be administered.

Missions –
1. The mandated services the Coast Guard performs in fulfilling its fundamental roles. Synonym: Duties. The Homeland Security Act (HSA) of 2002 lists 11 Coast Guard missions:

   - Ports, Waterways and Coastal Security (PWCS)
   - Drug Interdiction
   - Migrant Interdiction
   - Other Law Enforcement (foreign fisheries)
   - Living Marine Resources (domestic fisheries)
   - Marine Safety
   - Marine Environmental Protection
   - Ice Operations
   - Aids to Navigation (ATON)
   - Defense Readiness
   - Search and Rescue

2. Tasks or operations assigned to an individual or unit.

National Defense –

1. A collective term encompassing both the national defense and foreign relations of the United States. Specifically, the condition provided by a military or defense advantage over any foreign nation or group of nations.

2. A favorable foreign relations position.

3. A defense posture capable of successfully resisting hostile or destructive action from within or without, overt or covert.

National Defense Capabilities of the U.S. Coast Guard – from Memorandum of Agreement between the Department of Defense and the Department of Homeland Security on the Use of U.S. Coast Guard Capabilities and Resources in Support of the National Military Strategy–May 23, 2008

Military Environmental Response Operations – Response to oil discharges or hazardous material releases that could disrupt military operations of the U.S. and allied forces.

Port Operations Security and Defense – Operations conducted to ensure port and harbor areas are maintained free of hostile threats, terrorist actions, and safety deficiencies that would be a threat to deployment of military resources.

Theater Security Cooperation – All military activities involving other nations intended to shape the security environment in peacetime.

Coastal Sea Control Operations – Operations conducted to ensure the unimpeded use of designated offshore areas by U.S. and friendly forces and to deny the use of those areas by enemy forces.

Rotary Wing Air Intercept Operations – The use of helicopters to support national Air Defense. It includes alert, interception, communication, surveillance, and escort activities.

Combating Terrorism Operations – Operations to prevent and respond to terrorist acts. These may include anti-smuggling, migrant interdiction, counter-piracy, rule of law, counter-proliferation, and port security.

Maritime Operational Threat Response Support – Support to the integrated national-level maritime command centers to achieve coordinated, unified, timely, and effective U.S. government planning for, and response to, the full range of maritime security threats.

National Fleet – Outlined in the National Fleet Policy dated March 3, 2006, the U.S. National Fleet consists of the integrated and interoperable combined multi-mission assets of the U.S. Navy and the U.S. Coast Guard including ships, boats, aircraft, and shore command-and-control nodes. The National Fleet combined assets provide joint force multipliers to support the broad spectrum of national security requirements from power projection to security and defense of the homeland.

North Atlantic Coast Guard Forum – Initiated in 2007 as a venue to foster multilateral cooperation across the North Atlantic with European countries, Russia, and Canada through the sharing of information on matters related to combined operations, exchange of information, illegal drug trafficking, maritime security, fisheries enforcement, illegal migration, and maritime domain awareness.

North Pacific Coast Guard Forum – Initiated in 2000 as a venue and a role model for multinational cooperation and partnerships. It has similar goals to the North Atlantic Coast Guard Forum. The current membership includes agencies from Canada, China, Japan, Korea, Russia, and the United States.

Port State Control – The exercise of controls over a foreign vessel by the government of a nation within which the vessel is operating. The goal of port state control is to eliminate substandard ships, which pose a threat to life, property, and the marine environment.

Regulatory – Of or concerning a rule, law, order, or direction from a superior or competent authority regulating action or conduct.

Search and Rescue (SAR) – The use of available resources to assist persons and property in potential or actual distress. The Coast Guard is the lead agency for Maritime SAR. The Commandant has divided the Maritime SAR Area into two sections, the Atlantic Maritime Area and the Pacific Maritime Area. The Atlantic Area Commander is the Atlantic Area SAR Coordinator, and the Pacific Area Commander is the Pacific Area SAR Coordinator.

Specialized Service – An armed force specialized for a certain type or class of duties. The Coast Guard operates as a specialized service when part of the Navy.

Territorial Sea – Twelve nautical miles wide, and refers to the waters adjacent to the coast of the United States and seaward of the territorial sea baseline, which is normally the mean low water line. With respect to other nations, it refers to waters adjacent to that nation's coast that have a width and baseline recognized by the United States (normally 12 nautical miles wide). For a more comprehensive definition of Territorial Sea, see 33 CFR 2.22.

Appendix B: Alexander Hamilton's Report to the U.S. House of Representatives (Section V)

In early 1790, the U.S. House of Representatives directed the Secretary of the Treasury to report any difficulties his department may be experiencing in the execution of the "several laws for collecting duties on the goods, wares, and merchandises, and on tonnage, and for regulating the coasting trade, together with his opinion thereupon." (*Journal of the House*, I, 143.)

Hamilton's report of April 22, 1790, represents his first formal proposal for the "...few armed vessels, judiciously stationed at the entrances of our ports..." envisioned in Federalist Paper No. 12. In his report he makes his case to Congress for the construction and commissioning of 10 cutters.

More remarkably, his argument envisions a military, multi-mission and maritime service.

****

Report on Defects in the Existing Laws of Revenue

Treasury Department April 22nd, 1790.

[To the Speaker of the House of Representatives]

In obedience to the Order of the House of Representatives of the 19th Day of January last

The Secretary of the Treasury respectfully submits the following Report.

****

Section V. This Section [of the existing law] contemplates a provision of boats for securing the collection of the revenue; but no authority to provide them, is any where given. Information from several quarters, proves the necessity of having them; nor can they, in the opinion of the Secretary, fail to contribute, in a material degree, to the security of the revenue; much more than will compensate for the expence of the establishment; the utility of which will increase in proportion as the public exigencies may require an augmentation of the duties. An objection has been made to the measure as betraying an improper distrust of the Merchants; but that objection can have no weight, when it is considered, that it would be equally applicable to all the precautions comprehended in the existing system; all which proceed on a supposition too well founded to be doubted, that there are persons concerned in trade, in every country, who will, if they can, evade the public dues, for their private benefit. Justice to the body of the Merchants of the United States, demands an acknowledgement, that they have very generally manifested a disposition to conform to the national laws, which does them honor, and authorizes confidence in their probity. But every considerate member of that body, knows, that this confidence admits of exceptions, and that it is essentially the interest of the greater number, that every possible guard should be set on the fraudulent few; which does not in fact tend to the embarrassment of trade.

The following is submitted as a proper establishment for this purpose.

That there be ten boats: two, for the coasts, bays and harbours of Massachusetts and New Hampshire; one, for the Sound between Long-Island and Connecticut; one, for the Bay of New York; one, for the Bay of Delaware; two, for the Bay of Chesapeake; (these of course to ply along the neighboring coasts); one, for the coasts, bays and harbours of North Carolina; one, for the Coasts, bays and harbours of South Carolina; and one, for the Coasts, bays & harbours of Georgia.

Boats of from thirty six to forty feet keel, will answer the purpose, each having one Captain, one Lieutenant and six mariners, and armed with swivels. The first cost of one of these boats, completely equipped, may be computed at One thousand dollars.

The following is an estimate of the annual expence

10 Captains	@ 40. dollars per month	4,800
10 Lieutenants	@ 25. ditto per ditto	3,000
60 seamen	@ 8. ditto per ditto	5,760
Provision		3,000
Wear and Tear		2,000
	Dollars	18,560

The utility of an establishment of this nature must depend on the exertion, vigilance and fidelity of those, to whom the charge of the boats shall be confided. If these are not respectable characters, they will rather serve to screen, than detect fraud. To procure such, a liberal compensation must be given, and in addition to this, it will, in the opinion of the Secretary, be advisable, that they be commissioned as Officers of the Navy. This will not only induce fit men the more readily to engage, but will attach them to their duty by a nicer sense of honor.

Appendix C: Alexander Hamilton's Letter of Instruction to the Commanding Officers of Revenue Cutters — Circular of June 4, 1791

No other service or agency of the federal government ever received clearer sailing directions than did the Coast Guard from its founder, Alexander Hamilton. It is known that Hamilton had a deep and abiding concern as to the conduct of the crews. This is evidenced by his superbly written June 4, 1791 "Letter of Instruction" to the Captains of the first Revenue Cutters.

As Captain Commandant Horatio Davis Smith wrote in his early history of the U.S. Revenue Marine Service, "the Circular embodied the views of the Secretary concerning the Service he had created, the success of which was problematical, and over whose fortunes he watched with considerable solicitude. He was ever ready to listen to suggestions of officers tending to improve the Corps, and stood ready to aid the elevation and improvement of the Service by personal influence and the ready eloquence, of which he was such a complete master."

Today's principles of Coast Guard operations can be traced back to Hamilton's Circular of 1791. Hamilton set forth the conduct and operations he expected of his captains, officers, and cutters, and in doing so established the fundamental character of the U.S. Coast Guard. Over two centuries later, his "instructions" remain relevant to the Coast Guard and define our unique culture.

The following is the original text of that letter with a side-by-side modern English summary, by paragraph. **Coast Guard principles of operations are noted in *italics*.** The "Act" Hamilton refers to is the Act of Congress establishing the Revenue Marine, signed on August 4th, 1790—the date now recognized as the official birthday of the U.S. Coast Guard.

Alexander Hamilton's Letter of Instruction to the Commanding Officers of the Revenue Cutters

Treasury Department,
June 4th, 1791

Original Text of Letter	Modern English Summary
Sir:	Sir:
As you are speedily to enter upon the duties of your station it becomes proper briefly to point them out to you. Accordingly I send you a copy of the Act under which you have been appointed, and which are contained your powers and the objects to which you are to attend, and I shall add such observations as appears to me requisite to guide you in fulfilling the intent of that act.	Since you will soon begin your duties, I will briefly point them out to you. The enclosed Act contains your authorities and objectives. I will make some recommendations I believe will help guide you in fulfilling the intent of that act.
It may be observed generally that it will be in a partial manner, the province of the Revenue Cutter to guard Revenue laws from all infractions, or breaches, either upon the coasts or within the bays, or upon the rivers and other waters of the United States, previous to the anchoring of vessels within the harbors for which they are respectively destined.	As part of its job, the Revenue Cutter will enforce all Revenue laws upon the coasts, bays, rivers, or other waters of the United States prior to vessels anchoring in their port of arrival. (*Principle of clear objective*)
Hence, it will be necessary for you from time to time to ply along the coasts in the neighborhood of your station, and to traverse the different parts of the waters which it comprehends. To fix yourself constantly or even generally at one position, would in a great measure defeat the purpose of the establishment.	Hence, it will be necessary for you to actively patrol the coasts and waterways near your home port, covering all areas. To remain constantly, or even generally, in one particular spot would defeat the purpose of the Revenue Cutters and allow unlawful acts to occur everywhere else. (*Principle of effective presence*)

It would confine your vigilance to a particular spot, and allow full scope to fraudulent practices, everywhere else.

The 63d section of the act herewith transmitted, declared that the officers of the Revenue Cutters are to be deemed officers of the Customs, and enumerates certain powers with which they are to be invested. The 30th section treating of the same powers, that of demanding manifests and that of searching vessels, enters into some details concerning them. These sections require particular attention as marking the outline of authority and duty, but in the capacity of officers of the Customs you will possess some other powers, and be bound to perform some other duties which are not mentioned in those sections. You will have a right for examination, and it will be your duty to seize vessels and goods in the cases in which they are liable to seizure for breaches of the Revenue laws, when they come under your notice, but all the power you can exercise will be found in some provisions of the law and it must be a rule with you to exercise none with which you are not clearly invested. In every case of doubt you will follow the advice of the officer to whom you will be referred in a separate letter. On points of importance which admit of delay you may correspond with the Secretary of the Treasury.

Revenue Cutter officers are considered officers of the Customs. The Act gives you the authority to demand manifests and search vessels, but your capacity as officers of the Customs gives you some additional powers and duties. You have examination authority, and it will be your duty to seize vessels and goods, when appropriate, for violation of Revenue laws. All your authority comes from law, however, and you shall not act where you do not have clear authority. In every case of doubt you will follow the advice of the officer to whom you will be referred in a separate letter. [Note: These letters named local Collectors of Customs.] On urgent matters you may correspond directly with the Secretary of the Treasury. (*Principles of restraint and unity of effort*)

The 9th, 10th, 11th, and 12th sections which relate to manifests will also require your particular attention. The clear observance of the provisions of these sections is considered as of material consequences to the Secretary of the Treasury, and ample time having been allowed for them to be generally known and complied with, it is now indispensable that they should be strictly enforced.

Full compliance with the laws pertaining to vessel manifests is critical to the Secretary of the Treasury. Enough time has passed that these laws should be generally known and vessels should be in compliance. Therefore they should now be strictly enforced.

You will perceive that they are only required in respect to vessels belonging wholly or in part to a citizen or citizens, inhabitant or inhabitants of the United States. It is understood that by inhabitant is intended any person residing in the United States, whether citizen or foreign. The reason of the limitation is that citizens and resident foreigners are supposed to be acquainted with the laws of the country; but that foreign citizens residing in foreign countries, have not the same knowledge, and consequently ought not to be subjected to penalties in regard to a thing which they might not know to be necessary.

These laws pertaining to manifests apply only to vessels belonging wholly or in part to U.S. citizens, or resident foreign nationals. This does not include nonresident foreign citizens who cannot reasonably be expected to know, or be aware of, these laws.

But since you cannot be presumed to know beforehand what vessels are owned in whole or in part by citizens or inhabitants, it will, of course, be your duty to demand the manifests of all indiscriminately, and to report those from which you do not receive them, to the Collector of the District for which they are bound, and you will at the end

But since you cannot know the actual ownership of a vessel at sea, it is your duty to demand the manifest of all vessels. You shall report those vessels that do not supply you a proper manifest to the Collector of your District and submit an abstract of your records the Secretary of the Treasury at the end of each month.

of every month (pursuing the division of the year by the calendar) send me an abstract of your records.

Careful attention is likewise due to the 13th and 14th sections of the act. It is of importance that vessels should not break bulk, or put out any part of their cargo even temporarily, previous to a regular entry and permission obtained, except in cases of real necessity, to be duly reported and proved. You will observe that besides the penalties on the masters and mates of the vessels from on board of which any goods shall have been illegally removed, the master or commander of the vessel or boat into which they may be received, and all persons aiding in the removal, are liable to a forfeiture of treble the value of the goods removed, and the vessel or boat into which they may be received is also subject to forfeiture. It is well known that one of the most extensive cases of illicit trade is that which is here intended to be guarded against—that of unlading goods before the arrival of a vessel into port, in coasters and other small vessels, which convey them clandestinely to land. Hence, the bare removal of goods from one vessel to another is made penal, though they may not have been landed. Nor will the pretext of their being intended to be replaced avail anything. The provisions of these sections admonish you to keep a careful eye upon the motions of coasting vessels, without, however, inter-

It is illegal for vessels to offload any part of their cargo to shore or another vessel prior to regular entry and clearance, except in cases of real necessity that are reported and verified. In addition to the penalties for masters and mates of the supplying vessel, all violators and accomplices on a receiving vessel are liable to forfeiture of three times the value of the goods removed and forfeiture of their vessel. These provisions require you to keep a careful eye on coastwise vessels without, however, interrupting trade or embarrassing them unless your strong suspicion requires that they be boarded and examined. (*Principles of restraint*)

rupting or embarrassing them unless where some strong ground of suspicion requires that they should be visited and examined.

The execution of the 15th section of the Act essentially depends on the Revenue Cutters. It is easy to see that it would be dangerous to the revenue for vessels to be permitted to go at pleasure from one part of the United States to another without announcing themselves to some proper officer. Hence, though each may proceed on her voyage from a more exterior to a more interior district to which she may be bound—yet none can go back from a more interior to more exterior Districts, or from one part of the United States to another without first reporting himself to the Collector of the District, in order that he may come under the notice and precautions of the law. Nor can this be deemed a hardship; seeing her report will not oblige her to unlade any part of her cargo, but she may afterwards proceed with it wheresoever she pleases.

I have now noticed to you the principal parts of the law which immediately relate to the execution of your duty. It will, however, be incumbent upon you to make yourself acquainted with all the revenue laws, which concern foreign commerce, or the coasting trade—a knowledge of the whole spirit and tendency of which cannot but be a useful guide to you in your particular sphere.

Enforcement of law regarding the movement of vessels in U.S. waters depends on Revenue Cutters. We risk losing revenue if vessels move from one part of the United States to another, without proper notifications. Vessels may travel at will from more exterior Districts to more interior districts, but none can travel from more interior to more exterior Districts or from one state to another within the U.S. without first reporting to the Collector of the District.

I have pointed out certain parts of the law and your duties, but you must become familiar with all the revenue laws that concern foreign commerce or coastwise trade. Knowledge of the whole letter and spirit of these laws will be useful to you in carrying out your duties. The law allows officers of cutters, in certain cases, to remain aboard vessels until they arrive at their destination. Cutters have been

You will observe that the law contemplates the officers of cutters in certain cases remaining on board of vessels, until they arrive at their places of destination; and with a view to this it is that so many officers have been assigned to each cutter. It is not, however, expected that this will be done in every case, and it must be left to the discretion of the commanding officer when it shall be done—when there is a vessel, the lading of which is of very great value, or which has any considerable quantity of goods on deck, or in other situations from which they can readily be removed; or where the nature of the cargo is such as to admit more easily a clandestine landing, or from the highness of the duties to afford a more than ordinary temptation, or where a vessel is bound to a very interior district up long bays or rivers, or when any suspicious circumstances appear; in these and the like cases, it will be well to let an officer accompany the vessel to her place of destination. The want of a manifest will be a circumstance in favor of so doing. It will not, however, be advisable to make known the circumstances under which it is deemed most peculiarly proper to use these precautions; as it might sometimes unnecessarily give offense. It may be always left to be understood, that it is the practice whenever the state of the cutter renders it convenient. You are empowered, amongst other things, to affix seals on packages found in cer-

crewed accordingly. However, this should not occur in every case and it is left to the discretion of the commanding officer when it shall be done, based on circumstances and risk of violation of revenue law. Factors affecting risk include value of the cargo, the high value of the potential tax that would tempt someone to smuggle, situations where the cargo can be easily removed and smuggled ashore, a long transit to an interior district that would make smuggling easier, or other suspicious circumstances. A missing manifest could also justify placing an officer on the vessel. You do not need to advise the master why you are placing an officer onboard since that might unnecessarily offend them. Rather, you should make it clear that is the standard practice of the Cutter, when appropriate. You may also affix seals on packages to identify them later. (*Principles of on-scene initiative and managed risk*)

tain situations. For this purpose, proper seals will be prepared and transmitted. Till they are required, any other may be made use of. The principal design of this provision is to identify the packages found in such situations.

It will be expected that a regular journal be kept in each cutter, in the same manner, as far as circumstances are applicable, as is practiced in sea voyages, and that all occurrences, relative to the execution of the laws, and to the conduct of all vessels which come under their notice, be summarily noticed therein, and that a copy of this journal to the end of each month be regularly forwarded to the Treasury.

You shall keep a journal in each cutter that includes a summary of all law enforcement activities and the activity of all vessels contacted. A copy of this journal shall be forwarded to the Treasury at the end of each month.

It has also occurred that the cutters may be rendered an instrument of useful information, concerning the coast, inlets, bays and rivers of the United States, and it will be particularly acceptable if the officers improve the opportunities they have (as far as shall be consistent with the duties they are to perform) in making such observations and experiments in respect to the objects, as may be useful in the interests of navigation, reporting the result, from time to time to the Treasury.

As time permits, you are requested to gather information concerning the coasts, inlets, bays, and rivers of the U.S. as may be useful for navigation. You shall report these observations to the Treasury. **(*Principles of flexibility and unity of effort*)**

While I recommend in the strongest terms to the respective officers, activity, vigilance and firmness, I feel no less solicitude, that their deportment may be marked with prudence, moderation and good temper. Upon these last qualities,

While I recommend that all officers be active, vigilant, and firm, they must also be prudent, moderate, and good tempered. These last qualities are as important as the former, and will ensure the success of the Service. Officers must

not less that the former, must depend the success, usefulness and consequently continuance of the establishment in which they are included. They cannot be insensible that there are some pre-possessions against it, that the charge with which they are intrusted [sic] is a delicate one, and that it is easy by mismanagement, to produce serious and extensive clamour, disgust and odium.

They will always keep in mind that their countrymen are freemen, and, as such, are impatient of everything that bears the least mark of a domineering spirit. They will, therefore, refrain, with the most guarded circumspection, from whatever has the semblance of haughti-ness, rudeness, or insult. If obstacles occur, they will remember that they are under the particular protection of the laws and that they can meet with nothing disagreeable in the execu-tion of their duty which these will not severely reprehend. This reflection, and a regard to the good of the service, will prevent, at all times a spirit of irrita-tion or resentment. They will endeavor to overcome difficulties, if any are experienced, by a cool and temperate perseverance in their duty—by address and moderation, rather than by vehe-mence or violence. The former style of conduct will recommend them to the particular approbation of the President of the United States, while the reverse of it—even a single instance of outrage or intemperate or improper treatment of

keep in mind that some mariners will dislike their duties. The responsibility of officers in these duties is a delicate one and, if poorly managed, could easily upset people and result in complaints and con-demnation. (*Principle of restraint*)

Officers will always keep in mind that their fellow citizens are free, and, as such are impatient of anything that bears the least mark of a domineering spirit. They should carefully refrain from anything resembling arrogance, rudeness, or insult. If difficulties occur in the perfor-mance of their duties, they will remember they are under the protection of the laws and these laws will severely punish viola-tors. Knowing this, and keeping in mind the good of the Service, will prevent feel-ings of irritation or resentment in others. They will strive to overcome difficulties by a cool and even-tempered persever-ance in their duty—using conversation and moderation, rather than anger or violence. The former style of conduct is fully supported and encouraged by the President of the United States, while the latter—even a single instance of outrage, bad temper, or improper treatment of any person in the course of their duty—will meet with the President's pointed displea-sure and will have corresponding conse-quences. (*Principle of restraint*)

Appendix C: Hamilton's Letter of Instruction

any person with whom they have anything to do, in the course of their duty, will meet with his pointed displeasure, and will be attended with correspondent consequences.

The foregoing observations are not dictated by any doubt of the prudence of any of those to whom they are addressed. These have been selected with so careful an attention to character, as to afford the strongest assurance, that their conduct will be that of good officers and good citizens. But, in an affair so delicate and important, it has been judged most advisable to listen to the suggestions of caution rather than of confidence, and to put all concerned on their guard against those sallies to which even good and prudent men are occasionally subject. It is not doubted that the instructions will be received as it ought to be, and will have its due effect. And that all may be apprized [sic] of what is expected you will communicate this part of your orders, particularly, to all your officers, and you will inculcate upon your men a correspondent disposition.

The previous observations do not mean I doubt the judgment of any of the officers addressed. They have been selected with careful attention to their character, to ensure their conduct will reflect good officers and good citizens. But since our duties are so sensitive and important, I am urging all to be on their guard against outbursts and bad behavior that even good and prudent people occasionally have. You will communicate this particular part of the orders to all your officers, and you will teach and impress upon them a proper bearing. (*Principle of restraint*)

The 5th section of the Act, requires that all officers appointed pursuant to this Act, should take a certain oath therein specified. The Act of the 1st of June, 1789, requires that you should also take the oath to support the Constitution of the United States. These oaths, each of your officers must take before some

All Revenue Cutter officers must take the oath specified in this Act and must also take an oath to support the Constitution of the United States. These oaths must be taken before a Judge of the United States if one is convenient. If not, before some other magistrate empowered to administer oaths. A certificate of the taking of

Judge of the United States, if access can conveniently be had to one. If not, before some other magistrate, duly empowered to administer oaths, and a certificate from him, of the taking of it, must be transmitted to the Comptroller of the Treasury.

I am sir, your obedient servant,

ALEXANDER HAMILTON,
Secretary of the Treasury

this oath must be sent to the Comptroller of the Treasury.

I am sir, your obedient servant,

ALEXANDER HAMILTON,
Secretary of the Treasury

Appendix D: Campaign Streamers

The Stars and Stripes and the five standards of the U.S. Armed Forces, each with campaign streamers attached. The Coast Guard standard is on the far right.

Campaign Streamers* Earned 1790–1865:
Revenue Protection and More

1790–1797: Maritime Protection of the New Republic**

1798–1801: French Quasi-War

1812: War of 1812

1820–1861: African Slave Trade Patrol

1822–1830s: Operations against West Indian Pirates

1835–1842: The Indian Wars

1846–1848: Mexican War

1861–1865: The Civil War

Campaign Streamers Earned 1866–1914:
Expanding Duties for a Growing Nation

1898: Spanish-American War

Campaign Streamers Earned 1917–1946:
A Service Forged by War, Crisis, and Consolidation

1917–1918: World War I

1926–1927, 1930–1932: Yangtze Service

1939–1941: American Defense Service

1941–1942: Philippine Defense

1941–1946: World War II – American Theater

1941–1946: World War II – Pacific Theater

1941–1945: World War II – European-African-Middle Eastern Theater

1944–1945: Philippine Liberation

1941–1942, 1944–1945: Philippine Independence and Philippine Presidential Unit Citation

1945: World War II Victory

Other World War II Awards:

Croix de Guerre (France)

Presidential Unit Citation

Navy Occupation Service

Campaign Streamers Earned 1947–1972:
Sorting Out Roles and Missions.

1945–1957: China Service

1950–1954: Korean Service

1950–1954: National Defense Service Medal

1958–1965: Armed Forces Expeditionary

Campaign Streamers Earned 1973–2001:
A Unique Instrument of National Security

1962–1975: Vietnam Service

1970–1974: National Defense Service

1990–1995: National Defense Service

1991–1995: Southwest Asia Service

1994: Department of Transportation – Secretary's Outstanding Unit Award

Other Vietnam Service Awards:

Navy Unit Commendation

National Defense Service

Army Meritorious Unit Commendation

Navy Meritorious Unit Commendation

RVN Armed Forces Meritorious Unit Commendation, Gallantry Cross w/Palm

RVN Meritorious Unit Citation, Civil Actions Medal First Class Color w/Palm

Campaign Streamers Earned September 11, 2001, and Beyond: America's Maritime Guardian

1999–A closing date to be determined: Kosovo Campaign

2001–A closing date to be determined: National Defense Service

2001–A closing date to be determined: Global War on Terrorism Service

2001–A closing date to be determined: Global War on Terrorism Expeditionary

2001–A closing date to be determined: Afghanistan Campaign

2003–A closing date to be determined: Iraq Campaign

2005: Coast Guard Presidential Unit Citation

* For more information, look up "Campaign Streamers" in the Glossary (Appendix A).

** Awarded solely to the Coast Guard.

Appendix E: Further Reading

Headquarters Circular No. 126 of October 16, 1936 – There is a tendency to believe that current statements are original expressions of purpose and expectation, but in truth they are not. America's Maritime Guardian is not the first authoritative statement of Coast Guard doctrine. In 1936, for example, Headquarters Circular No. 126 laid down doctrine that with minimum editing (largely to update our mission set) would be as applicable today as it was more than 60 years ago.

Strategic Planning Documents – America's Maritime Guardian describes what we do, why we do it, and who we are as an organization. It does not describe the challenges we face as a nation and Service, our vision for the future, our goals to reach that future, or when and how we plan to reach our goals. These subjects are addressed in the following strategic planning documents.

- Current National Security Strategy
- Current National Military Strategy
- Current National Strategy for Homeland Security
- National Strategy for Maritime Security (and Supporting Plans) September 2005
- A Cooperative Strategy for 21ˢᵗ Century Seapower, October 2007
- Current Department of Homeland Security, Strategic Plan
- Report of the Interagency Task Force on U.S. Coast Guard Roles and Missions. *A Coast Guard for the Twenty First Century.* December 1999

Service Doctrine – The following two publications serve as capstone doctrine for the joint forces and U.S. Navy, respectively.

- *Joint Publication 1, Doctrine for the Armed Forces of the United States,* May 14, 2007
- *Naval Doctrine Publication 1 – Naval Warfare,* March 28, 1994

History – America's Maritime Guardian provides a brief overview of the rich history of the Coast Guard and its predecessor organizations. A better knowledge of the history of the Coast Guard, as contained in the following recommendations, will enhance the reader's understanding of our Service. The Coast Guard Historian's Office also maintains a list of the best books on Coast Guard history in print.

- Beard, Barrett Thomas. *Wonderful Flying Machines: A History of U.S. Coast Guard Helicopters.* Annapolis: U.S. Naval Institute Press, 1996.
- Browning, Robert M., Jr. "The Coast Guard Captains of the Port," in Jan M. Copes and Timothy Runyon, ed., *To Die Gallantly: The Battle of the Atlantic.* New York: Westview Press, 1994.
- Clifford, Mary Louise and Dennis Noble. *Rescued By the U.S. Coast Guard: Great Acts of Heroism Since 1878.* Annapolis: U.S. Naval Institute Press, 2004.
- Evans, Stephen H. *The United States Coast Guard, 1790-1915:* A Definitive History. Annapolis: U.S. Naval Institute Press, 1949.
- Frump, Robert. *Until the Sea Shall Free Them.* Garden City: Doubleday, 2001.
- Frump, Robert. *Two Tankers Down: The Greatest Small-Boat Rescue in U.S. Coast Guard History.* Guilford: Lyons Press, 2008.
- Johnson, Robert Erwin. *Guardians of the Sea: History of the United States Coast Guard, 1915 to the Present.* Annapolis: U.S. Naval Institute Press, 1987.
- King, Irving H. *George Washington's Coast Guard: Origins of the U.S. Revenue Cutter Service, 1789-1801.* Annapolis: U.S. Naval Institute Press, 1978.
- King, Irving H. *The Coast Guard Expands, 1865-1915.* Annapolis: U.S. Naval Institute Press, 1996.

- King, Irving H. *The Coast Guard Under Sail: The U.S. Revenue Cutter Service, 1789-1865.* Annapolis: U.S. Naval Institute Press, 1989.
- Junger, Sebastian. *The Perfect Storm.* New York: W.W. Norton, 1997.
- Kroll, C. Douglas. *Commodore Ellsworth P. Bertholf: first Commandant of the Coast Guard.* Annapolis: U.S. Naval Institute Press, 2002.
- LaGuardia-Kotite, Martha. *So Others May Live: Coast Guard Rescue Swimmers: Saving Lives, Defying Death (Foreword by Governor Tom Ridge).* Guilford: The Lyons Press, 2006.
- Larzelere, Alex. *The Coast Guard at War.* Annapolis: U.S. Naval Institute Press, 1997.
- Noble, Dennis L. *Lifeboat Sailors: Disasters, Rescues, and the Perilous Future of the Coast Guard's Small Boat Stations.* Washington, DC: Brassey's, 2000.
- Noble, Dennis L. *Lighthouses & Keepers: The U.S. Lighthouse Service and Its Legacy.* Annapolis: U.S. Naval Institute Press, 1997.
- Noble, Dennis L. *That Others Might Live: The U.S. Life-Saving Service, 1878-1915.* Annapolis: U.S. Naval Institute Press, 1994.
- Noble, Dennis L. and Truman R. Strobridge. *Alaska and the U.S. Revenue Cutter Service, 1867-1915.* Annapolis: U.S. Naval Institute Press, 1999.
- President of the United States, Assistant to the President for Homeland Security and Counterterrorism. *Federal Response to Hurricane Katrina: Lessons Learned, February 2006.* Washington, DC: U.S. Government Printing Office, 2006.
- *They Had to Go Out: True Stories of American's Coastal Life-Savers From the Pages of "Wreck & Rescue Journal."* Hull: United States Life-Saving Service Heritage Association, 2007.
- U.S. Coast Guard. *International Ice Patrol.* Washington, DC: U.S. Department of Transportation, July 1984.
- Walling, Michael. *Bloodstained Sea: The U.S. Coast Guard in the Battle of the Atlantic, 1941-1944.* International Marine/Ragged Mountain Press, 2004.
- Wiley, Ken. *Lucky Thirteen: D-Days in the Pacific with the U.S. Coast Guard in World War II.* Drexel Hill: Casemate Publishing, 2007.
- Willoughby, Malcolm F. *The U.S. Coast Guard in World War II.* New York: Arno Printing, 1980.

Maritime Policy – The Coast Guard not only executes U.S. maritime policy, we also play a significant role in the development of that policy. The following are excellent books on maritime policy issues.

- *America's Living Oceans: Charting a Course for Sea Change.* Pew Oceans Commission, 2003.
- *An Ocean Blueprint for the 21st Century.* U.S. Commission on Ocean Policy, 2004.
- Baur, Donald. *Ocean and Coastal Law and Policy.* Chicago: American Bar Association, 2008.
- Freestone, David et.al. *The Law of the Sea.* Oxford Oxfordshire: Oxford University Press, 2006.
- Fuss, Charles M., Jr. and W.T. Leland. *Sea of Grass.* Annapolis: U.S. Naval Institute Press, 1996.
- McNicholas, Michael. *Maritime Security.* Oxford: Butterworth-Heinemann, 2007.
- Stevenson, Charles. *Warriors and Politicians.* New York: Routledge, 2006.
- Till, Geoffrey. *Seapower: A Guide to the Twenty-First Century.* London: Frank Cass, 2004.

Leadership – The Coast Guard has a long history of developing strong leaders. The following book describes how the Coast Guard creates, instills, and maintains leadership throughout the Service.

- Phillips, Donald T. and ADM James M. Loy, USCG (Ret.). *Character in Action: The U.S. Coast Guard on Leadership*. Annapolis: U.S. Naval Institute Press, 2003.

Other recommended leadership books include:

- Abrashoff, D. Michael. *It's Your Ship*. New York: Warner Books, 2002.
- Bennis, Warren. *On Becoming a Leader*. Cambridge: Perseus Pub, 2003.
- Chernow, Ron. *Alexander Hamilton*. New York: Penguin Press, 2005.
- Collins, Jim. *Good to Great*. New York: Harper Collins Publishers Inc, 2001.
- Cowley, Michael and Ellen Domb. *Beyond Strategic Vision*. Newton: Butterworth-Heinemann, 1997.
- Ensher, Ellen A. and Susan B. Murphy. *Power Mentoring*. San Francisco: Jossey-Bass, 2005.
- Kaplan, Robert S. and David P. Norton. *The Strategy-Focused Organization*. Boston: Harvard Business School Press, 2001.
- Kotter, John P. and Dan S. Cohen. *The Heart of Change*. Boston: Harvard Business School Press, 2002.
- Malone, Dandridge. *Small Unit Leadership*. Novato: Presidio Press, 1983.
- Patterson, Kerry et.al. *Crucial Confrontations*. New York: McGraw-Hill, 2004.
- Phillips, Donald and ADM James M. Loy. *The Architecture of Leadership*. Annapolis: U.S. Naval Institute Press, 2008.
- Phillips, Donald T. *The Founding Fathers on Leadership*. New York: Warner Books, 1998.
- Sample, Steven. *The Contrarian's Guide to Leadership*. San Francisco: Jossey-Bass, 2003.
- Wouk, Herman. *The Caine Mutiny: A Novel of World War II*. Boston: Little, Brown, 1992.

Legal Authorities – The Coast Guard has been granted broad legal authority to act. The following publication outlines the numerous sources of that authority.

- Coast Guard Legal Authorities, COMDTPUB P5850.2 (series)

Endnotes

1   The five roles (maritime safety, maritime security, national defense, maritime mobility, and protection of natural resources) found in the previous version of Coast Guard Publication 1 and in other previous Coast Guard planning documents have now been grouped into maritime safety, security, and stewardship by the organization. As such, the role of maritime security encompasses both traditional maritime security and national defense activities, and the role of maritime stewardship encompasses activities for maritime mobility and the protection of natural resources. The Coast Guard's eleven mandated missions fall within the roles of maritime safety, security, and stewardship.

2   This estimate includes both registered and unregistered boats.

3   At the beginning of 2008, there were 40,698 Active Duty Coast Guard members and 7,396 full-time Coast Guard civilian employees.

4   At the beginning of 2008, there were 7,992 Coast Guard Selected Reserves and 2,795 Coast Guard Individual Ready Reserves.

5   At the beginning of 2008, there were 28,443 Coast Guard Auxiliary members.

6   At the end of 2008, there were 198,902 active duty U.S. Marines.

7   Stephen H. Evans. *The United States Coast Guard, 1790-1915: A Definitive History* (Annapolis: U.S. Naval Institute, 1949) 5 [hereafter Evans, Definitive History of the Coast Guard].

8   Quoted in Robert Erwin Johnson, *Guardians of the Sea* (Annapolis: U.S. Naval Institute Press, 1987) 1.

9   Evans, *Definitive History of the Coast Guard*, 13.

10   Act of August 4, 1790 (1 Stat. L., 145, 175) (Ten per cutter–a master, three mates, four mariners and two boys.)

11   Dennis L. Noble, *Lighthouses and Keepers: The U.S. Lighthouse Service and its Legacy* (Annapolis: U.S. Naval Institute Press, 1997) 7 There were at least 11 lighthouses before the revolution, but the first one is generally agreed to have been the Boston Light, located on Little Brewster Island, Boston Harbor, Massachusetts, Id., 5.

12   Act of August 7, 1789 (1 Stat. L, 53).

13   Evans, *Definitive History of the Coast Guard*, 4.

14   Act of July 7, 1797 (1 Stat. L. 523,525).

15   Johnson, *Guardians of the Sea*, 2.

16   Act of December 22, 1837 (5 Stat. L. 208).

17   Act of July 7, 1838 (5 Stat. L. 304), Quoted in Evans, *Definitive History of the Coast Guard*, 29.

18   Evans, *Definitive History of the Coast Guard*, 29.

19   Joshua M. Smith, *"'So Far from the Eye of Authority': The Embargo of 1807 and the U.S. Navy, 1807-1809,"* in William B. Cogar (ed.), New Interpretations in Naval History: Selected Papers from the Twelfth Naval History Symposium (Annapolis: U.S. Naval Institute Press, 1996), 132.

20   For an excellent treatment of this subject, see Warren S. Howard, *American Slavers and the Federal Law, 1837-1862* (Berkeley: University of California Press, 1963).

21   Quoted in *The U.S. Coast Guard: A Historical Overview* by the Office of the Coast Guard Historian.

22   Evans, *Definitive History of the Coast Guard*, 76.

23   President Lincoln invoked the provisions of section 98 of *An Act to Regulate the Collection of Duties on Imports and Tonnage,* March 2, 1799, which stated that "revenue cutter shall, whenever the President of the United States shall so direct, co-operate with the Navy of the United States, during which time, they shall be under the direction of the Secretary of the Navy…". Stat. L., 626, 699-700.

24   Evans, *Definitive History of the Coast Guard*, p. 75, citing Army and Navy Journal, November 26, 1864. This claim was verified by Captain (E) J. H. Pulsifer, USCG (Ret.) in the U. S. C. G. Association Journal, 1917, Vol. 1, No. 1.

25   For many decades the Service had no official title, although "Revenue Marine" or "Revenue Service" seem to have been the most common appellations in the 1800s. Not until 1863 did Congress actually call the Service by name. In that year, Congress used the name in *An Act in Relation to Commissioned Officers of the United States Revenue Cutter Service*, February 4, 1863, 12 Stat. L. 639.

26   Irving H. King, *The Coast Guard Expands, 1865-1915: New Roles, New Frontiers* (Annapolis: U.S. Naval Institute Press, 1996), 11-13.

27   Id., 13.

28   In 1872, the fleet consisted of 35 cutters, of which 25 were steamers. Id., 14. In 1881, the numbers were 36 and 31, respectively. Id., 17.

29   Joe A. Mobely, *Ship Ashore! The U.S. Lifesavers of Coastal North Carolina* (Raleigh, NC: North Carolina Department of Cultural resources, Division of Archives and History, 1994), 26-27.

30   For a discussion of the *Huron* and *Metropolis* disasters and their effect, see Mobley, *Ship Ashore!*, 53-90.

31   This task was the precursor to those associated with Maritime Defense Zones during the late twentieth century.

32 Evans, Definitive History of the Coast Guard, 169-72. In his letter to Congress, the President wrote:

> On the 11th of May, 1898, there occurred a conflict in the Bay of Cardenas, Cuba in which the naval torpedo boat Winslow was disabled, her commander wounded, and one of her officers and a part of her crew killed by the enemy's fire. In the face of a most galling fire from the enemy's guns the revenue cutter Hudson, commanded by First Lieutenant Frank H. Newcombe, [USRCS], rescued the disabled Winslow, her wounded commander and remaining crew. The commander of the Hudson kept his vessel in the very hottest fire of the action...until he finally [was able to tow] that vessel out of range of the enemy's guns, a deed of special gallantry. Id., 171-2.

33 Johnson, *Guardians of the Sea*, 232.

34 King, *The Coast Guard Expands*, 232.

35 Coast Guard aviation traces its beginnings to 1915, when Lieutenants Elmer F. Stone and Norman B. Hall of the cutter Onondaga persuaded Captain Benjamin M. Chiswell to allow them to fly search missions for the cutter in a borrowed aircraft. Their successes led Congress to authorize a fledgling aviation program, but Congress failed to follow up with appropriations. The program lay dormant until after World War I, when the Coast Guard established an air station in Morehead City, North Carolina, using an abandoned naval air station and borrowed Navy flying boats. Again, the failure of appropriations doomed the program, and the air station closed in 1922. Johnson, *Guardians of the Sea*, 42, 67.

36 P.L. 755, June 22, 1936, 49 Stat. 1820. The law did not apply on the inland waters of the United States, except the Great Lakes and their connecting waters.

37 During World War II, even the reserves required augmentation in order to meet port security needs. In June 1942, the Coast Guard established a Temporary Reserve made up of men and women who were excluded from full-time military service. By 1944, 50,000 served, primarily as a part-time Volunteer Port Security Force. Robert M. Browning, Jr. *Captains of the Port* (Washington, DC: Coast Guard Historians Office, 1993), 15-16.

38 Id., 177.

39 Id., 195-196.

40 Id., 220-22. The acronym LORAN, adopted to conceal the project from our enemies, was a shortened version of "Long Range Navigation." Id., 221.

41 Alex Larzelere, *The Coast Guard at War: Vietnam 1965–1975* (Annapolis: U.S. Naval Institute Press, 1997), 7.

42 Id., 121.

43 Originally known as the "Atlantic Merchant Vessel Emergency reporting System," AMVER became operational on July 18, 1958.

44 Johnson, *Guardians of the Sea*, 341.

45   The Timber Reserve Act of 1822, 3 Stat. L. 651 (February 23, 1822) authorized the President to "employ so much of the land and naval forces of the United States" as necessary to preserve public lands of live oak, used to build the stout hulls of men-o'war, located in Florida. According to Evans, the Revenue Marine enforced this law. Evans, *Definitive History of the Coast Guard*, 29.

46   Act of March 3, 1899, ch. 425, § 13, 30 Stat. 1152 codified at 33 U.S. Code § 407.

47   The three forward deployed fleets are the Fifth Fleet in the Arabian Gulf/Middle East, the Sixth Fleet in the Mediterranean, and the Seventh Fleet in the Western Pacific.

48   From Title 14 U.S. Code, Section 1.

49   Interagency Task Force Report on Coast Guard Roles and Missions, *A Coast Guard for the Twenty First Century*, December 3, 1999, ix.

50   Source: Chadwick, J. 1973. *Documents in Mycenaean Greek, 2nd ed.*, Cambridge as referenced by Kalliopi Efkleido, Department of Classics, University of Cincinnati, November 19, 2004.

51   From ALCOAST 039/94.

52   10 U.S. Code § 5062.

53   The prohibition is statutory for the Army and Air Force (Act of June 18, 1878, ch. 263, § 15, 20 Stat. L. 145, 152; codified at 18 U.S. Code § 1385) and it is a matter of Secretary of Defense policy for the Navy and Marine Corps (See Department of Defense Directive 5525.5). It does not apply to the Coast Guard.

54   Annual report of the U.S. Coast Guard for the Fiscal Year ended June 30, 1915, Government Printing Office, Washington, DC, 1915, Treasury Department Document No. 2746, Coast Guard 45.

55   The previous version of *Coast Guard Pub 1* contained two appendices that are not found in this version (i.e., *The Principles of War* and *The Principles of Military Operations Other Than War*). In 2006, *Joint Publication 3-0: Joint Operations* combined the nine *Principles of War* with three principles taken from *Military Operations Other Than War* to form the 12 Principles of Joint Operations:

Principles of War	*OtherPrinciples*
• Objective	• Restraint
• Offensive	• Perseverance
• Mass	• Legitimacy
• Economy of Force	
• Maneuver	
• Unity of Command	
• Security	
• Surprise	
• Simplicity	

These 12 principles are described in *Joint Pub 3-0* and are better suited for discussion and treatment within the future *Coast Guard Publication 3-0* that will describe Coast Guard operational doctrine. *Joint Pub 3-0* also discontinued the use of the acronym "military operations other than war (MOOTW)" and superseded *Joint Pub 3-07: Joint Doctrine for Military Operations Other Than War*, June 16, 1995.

56   Alexander Hamilton, Letter of Instruction, June 4, 1791, ¶ 3.

57   Irving H. King, The Coast Guard Expands 1865-1915, (Annapolis: U.S. Naval Institute Press, 1996), 8, 198.

58   Hamilton, Letter of Instruction, ¶ 14.

> *This publication is not intended to, and does not, create any right, benefit, standard, substantive or procedural, enforceable at law or in equity by any party against the United States of America, its departments, agencies, or entities, its officers, employees, or agents, or any other person.*

Following Page: Coast Guard emblem on the gates of Arlington National Cemetary.